Co-Missioned

The Story of Two People Who Went

by Betty Byrd

Acknowledgement

Sincere appreciation goes to Carla Williams and Shauna Raymer. Carla gave me the courage to attempt this project. Thank you, Carla, for the hours spent listening, asking questions, transcribing, and editing. Shauna made the work look beautiful! Her design and layout made me think all of these words really did make a book and gave me the hope to keep working past the second draft. Thank you, Shauna.

For copies of this book or more information, please contact:
Betty Byrd
5517 Cannonwood Drive
Louisville, KY 40229
bbyrd@teamexpansion.org

A portion of the proceeds from this book will go toward the funding of future development of Team Expansion's prayer, retreat, and learning center at Emerald Hills in Louisville, KY.

WORLDWIDE PUBLISHING GROUP
Your Multi-Platform Publishing Partner
(713) 766-4272

EBook: 978-1-312-65577-5
Softcover: 978-1-312-65575-1
Hardcover: 978-1-312-65576-8

Published in the United States of America

Dedication

This book is dedicated to the loving memory of my husband
Cecil Curtis Byrd
October 6, 1943 – January 20, 2000
Life would have been only half the journey without him...

And
to our children who went with us from the beginning of the journey....
Benjamin Curtis Byrd
Miriam Jannette Byrd Hans

And
to our children who joined us along the way....
Kathryn Elizabeth Byrd Willingham
Daniel Wells Byrd
Deborah Eloise Byrd Knierim

And, above all, **Jesus**, who said,
"Go ye therefore, and make disciples of all nations,
baptizing them in the name of the Father, and the Son, and of the Holy Ghost:
Teaching them to observe all things whatsoever I commanded you:
and, lo, I am with you always, even unto the end of the world. Amen."
(Matthew 28: 19-20 KJV)

And he said unto them,
"Go ye into all the world and preach the gospel to every creature."
(Mark 16:15 KJV)

May God be glorified.

Introduction

The purpose of this book is to chronicle the journey and experiences of two people who came to be known as missionaries.

They were ordinary people --
    from ordinary places --

And they followed the most extraordinary God.

May those who read these pages be inspired to listen to and act upon the call of this same God, the Father of our Lord and Savior, Jesus Christ, in their own lives.

To God be the glory.

Table of Contents

Go!

Who, Me?

The Hardest Part

Go.....to move or proceed to or from something; to leave a place; depart
Go.....a simple, two-lettered command
But how simple is it to move or proceed from one place to another?
How simple is it to leave a place
    to leave a home
    to leave a friend
    to leave a family
    to leave a mother
    to leave a father
    to leave a daughter
    to leave a son and two daughters
    to leave a son-in-law
    to leave a daughter-in-law
    to leave a granddaughter
    to leave two granddaughters
    to leave three granddaughters?
Going only got harder as the years progressed.

The most profound lesson that I learned in 24 years of service overseas is that the hardest aspect of being a missionary is obedience to the first word of the command that Jesus gave to those who would be the "sent out" ones. The teaching, the preaching, the language learning, the acculturation, the daily living, and the being there -- they all fall into place. It is the word "go" that can trip one up. It is the going that is the hurdle.

How ironic this is to those who view a missionary as a privileged world-traveler – one who gets to go see places, do things, have adventures.

I must admit that as a young girl, and then as a young woman, I looked forward to the going. From as far back as high school days, I dreamed of going to Africa as a missionary. As a young wife and mother, I was excited that we were going to the Dark Continent.

How oblivious I had been to my mother's tears my senior year in high school. I couldn't wait to go. My mother, on the other hand, viewed my going to college as the final preparation for the final separation.

In the years that followed, I was again oblivious to the pain of my parents. It was not until ten years later, September 12, 1976, the day on which Cecil and I were to depart for Zambia the first time, that I began to feel an inkling of what it meant to go. My father, who was supposed to drive us from Roanoke Rapids, North Carolina, to the airport in Richmond, Virginia, lay on his bed – paralyzed with grief that we were going. In the end, he was so overcome with grief that my sister had to drive us while my dad remained behind.

Still, the full impact of going did not hit me. It was not until sixteen years later when we pulled out of the drive-way of the mission house in which we had been furloughing, leaving our first daughter, who was expecting her first child, standing in tears beside her husband, that I finally knew the cost of going. Four years later, when we left our second daughter in the same driveway, the price of going had become even greater. In the years that followed, the expense of going doubled and doubled and doubled again.

In order to obey the command to go, we were called upon to move from the United States and proceed to Africa. No easy task. One step at a time, we obeyed. First, we moved from Kentucky to Oklahoma for linguistics training. At that time, we sold or gave away all of our earthly possessions (which consisted of a sofa, a chair, a bed, and a dresser). We sold the bedroom furniture and gave away the living room furniture to the man who mobilized us to go.

The eventual move to Africa required a year and a half of support-raising, the acquisition of airline tickets, and the shipping of crates. Oh, what it takes to go!

Long ago, God said to Abram, "Leave your country, your people, and your household and go to the land I will show you." (Genesis 12:1 NIV)

God had told us to leave the country and people with whom we were familiar, to leave our parents and siblings, and proceed to a country that we had never seen.

How did we know that God was telling us to go?

The Call

Whom Does God Call?

Whenever God calls me to do something that I don't feel capable of doing, I think about Moses. God asked Moses to go to Pharaoh to deliver the Israelites out of Egypt. Moses immediately asked God, "Who am I that I should go to Pharaoh and bring the Israelites out of Egypt?" (Exodus 3:11 NIV)

God promised to be with Moses, but Moses was still apprehensive about the whole deal. He wanted to know: What shall I say? What if they don't believe me? So God told him what to say – even gave him signs to prove that he was on a mission for God.

Then Moses came up with more excuses: "I have never been eloquent...I am slow of speech and tongue." (Exodus 4:10 NIV)

God promised to help him speak and to teach him what to say.

Then Moses begged, "O Lord, please send someone else to do it." (Exodus 4:13 NIV)

Moses is a prime example of the kind of person God uses – the unconfident, the non-eloquent, the reluctant, the one who is fearful of failing.

Paul explained this concept in I Corinthians 1:27 (NIV) "But God chose the foolish things of this world to shame the wise; God chose the weak things of the world to shame the strong."

Again in II Corinthians 12:9, 10 (NIV): "But he said to me, 'My grace is sufficient for you, for my power is made perfect in weakness.' Therefore I will boast all the more gladly about my weaknesses, so that Christ's power may rest on me. That is why, for Christ's sake, I delight in weaknesses, in insults, in hardships, in persecutions, in difficulties. For when I am weak, then I am strong."

God chooses the most unlikely vessels through whom to do His work. That's why He chose me. That's why He chose Cecil.

Betty's Call

What would ever possess us to leave our fathers and mothers and brothers and sisters and families and homes and all that was familiar?

It was the call of God upon our lives.

For me, the call came soon after I accepted Christ as my Savior. I was twelve years old, in the seventh grade. I had wanted to step out into that aisle at church for awhile before I ever did it. It was mostly fear that held me back.

From the time I was a young child, I had loved going to church. My mother had taken me even when I was nursery age. I remember being in the Beginners Class with Mrs. Gray and Mrs. Riggins. I remember when they told us that we were Gentiles. That made an impression on me because, until that time, I thought I was just a Tarheel. Billy Reaves questioned Mrs. Riggins about that. She said being a Gentile was different from being a Tarheel. That stuck.

I remember my Rainbow Bible. It had a picture of Jesus and the little children on the cover. It taught me that Jesus loved me. I loved looking at the glossy pictures in it and reading the Bible words. One day, I was asked to memorize my favorite verse for a Vacation Bible School program. At that time, I hadn't memorized much Scripture, so I opened my Rainbow Bible, and the pages fell to Psalm 40:1 (NIV). It read, "I waited patiently for the

Lord; he turned to me and heard my cry. He lifted me out of the slimy pit, out of the mud and mire; he set my feet on a rock and gave me a firm place to stand."

From that day forward, I knew God was doing that for me.

In the sixth grade, my Sunday school teacher shamed me into going to Christian service camp. She said everyone else was going; why wasn't I? Well, really it was because I didn't want to leave home, but how could I say that in front of the whole Sunday school class? So, I said I would go.

Once I got there, I wasn't very fond of it. Not being very athletic, I didn't like playing softball and volleyball every afternoon. I never seemed to connect with either ball at the right time -- not with my hands, nor with a bat, nor with a glove. But I did like our morning quiet times, the Bible classes, and the vesper services. They drew me closer and closer to Jesus. I wanted to go forward at the end of the vesper services and be baptized in the river after the Friday night campfire, but I never stepped forward. I was scared.

A few months later, in October, we had a revival at church. I went every night. My friends Gwynnell, Doris, and Marie said I should come forward during the revival and be baptized (they had already done so a few years before). I told my parents that I wanted to be a Christian. Then I stepped forward one night (October 12, 1960) and was baptized into Christ. I was a new creature. There was no turning back.

I was turned on for Jesus! I was hungry and thirsty for Him -- couldn't get enough of Sunday school, youth group, Sunday morning and Sunday evening worship services, Wednesday evening prayer meetings, youth revivals, youth rallies, fall revivals, Vacation Bible School, and special times when missionaries would come to speak. I remember when a husband and wife came to tell about the uprising in the Congo. A single woman missionary, Phyllis Rhine, was killed. That made an impression on me. I began to think about what it meant to give one's life in service to God.

By the time I was 16, I had been back to camp four times -- still loved the learning times and hated the recreation times. I never did get any better at hitting or catching a softball or a volleyball. The last time I attended camp was for Life Recruit Week.

When I was growing up in North Carolina, young people were encouraged to dedicate their lives to full-time Christian service. Those who did became members of Life Recruit Clubs. I wanted to do that -- not to be a member of a club but to seal an agreement with God that I would dedicate my life to full-time Christian service. I was totally convinced, actually from the time that I was baptized, that what else would, could, or should I want to do with my life except somehow work in full-time Christian service. I took the Great Commission very seriously. I thought, "Oh, Jesus didn't just say those words to the disciples; He gave that command to all of us."

On top of that, I was so grateful for what Christ had done for me. I thought, "The least I can do in return would be to work somehow for Him."

There was a song around that time that expressed how I felt. It was called,

"To God Be the Glory." I think Andrae Crouch is responsible for the song and the lyrics, but I first heard it when Mike Berry sang it. He was a young man from my hometown who went to Cincinnati Bible College and made a record with the song on it. These are the words:

How can I say thanks for the things you have done for me?
Things so undeserved yet you gave to prove your love for me?
The voices of a million angels cannot express my gratitude.
All that I am and ever hope to be, I owe it all to you.

To God be the glory, to God be the glory.
To God be the glory for the things He has done.
With His blood, He has saved me.
By His power, He has raised me.
To God be the glory for the things He has done.

Just let me live my life, and let it be pleasing, Lord, to Thee.
And should I gain any praise, let it go to Calvary.
With His blood, He has saved me.
By His power, He has raised me.
To God be the glory for the things He has done.

Between that song and the story of Phyllis Rhine, I knew that there was nothing else I could do with my life other than consecrate it to God's service. When He had done so much for me, how could I do any less than give my all for Him? So, I walked down the aisle and dedicated my life to full-time Christian service.

I dreamed of the day I could go to Bible college and begin training to be a missionary. A quartet of young men from Johnson Bible College held a youth revival at my home church. I remembered the sermon from the words of Peter concerning being a peculiar people, a royal priesthood. That's what I wanted to be. Africa was still on my mind. I read the newsletters that arrived from those serving on that continent. I was living in the 60s -- the decade of missions in Africa. God was moving me in that direction. I just needed to follow one step at a time.

His ways are not always our ways, nor His timing our timing. I moved forward as best I could -- entered Bible college, studied hard, worked hard, and looked forward to going to Africa. And then Cecil Byrd arrived on campus.

I was in love, and I was confused. Cecil had never said a word about going to Africa. Was God un-calling me? How could that be?

Cecil's Call

Cecil ended up on the campus of Johnson Bible College in an entirely different way than I had. He came via California where he had been living for several years. With a beer in one hand and a cigarette in the other, he was watching TV as the funeral train carrying the body of Bobby Kennedy made its way across country. For some reason, the thought came to his mind, "Where would my soul be headed if my dead body was on that train?"

He knew good and well where his soul would be headed, and it wouldn't be to Heaven. He made a decision right then to turn his life over to God, move back to Virginia where his family was living, and become a preacher. He thought he would be unable to stay faithful to God unless he was in ministry.

Cecil was no stranger to ministry. Bruce Rockwell, a young Baptist minister in Spencer, Virginia, and his wife, Mary Frances, had taken Cecil into their home in Cecil's late teenaged years. They literally took him right out of jail and promised to be responsible for him while he finished high school. Spencer is one of those very small communities in which everyone knows everyone else. The Byrd family was particularly well-known because of the four handsome, athletic boys and the tragedy of their mother's death in an automobile accident.

The Rockwells treated Cecil as if he was their own son, an older brother to their young children. They had rules: no drinking, no smoking, and no breaking curfew. There were chores to be done, too, like mowing the grass, -- and no going out until you did, and no going out on school nights, either. Get that homework done, boy! And you'd better be in church on Sunday! And that he was.

Those years living with the Rockwells were a formative time in Cecil's life. He even managed to graduate from high school during those two years -- a couple of years later than most in his class, but "better late than never," as the old saying goes.

Once he was out from under Bro. Rockwell's supervision, he returned to his wicked ways. The Gospel seeds, however, had been planted. Having been under the influence of Bro. Rockwell as a Baptist minister and having been baptized at Mayo Baptist Church during the time he lived in the Rockwell home, Cecil left California and returned to Virginia in hopes of enrolling in a Baptist college.

His plans changed when his sister, Sharon, introduced him to Vernon Eaton, the young minister at Morgan Ford Christian Church in Ridgeway, Virginia. Vernon, also known as Butch, told Cecil about Johnson Bible College, the college from which he had recently graduated. He called the college and secured a place for Cecil. Just like that!

A few days later, with nine dollars in his pocket, waiting on the side of the road for Walter Thornton to give him a ride to Johnson Bible College,

15

Cecil smoked his last cigarette.

God's call on Cecil's life was just beginning. Little did he know that the next steps would lead to Africa.

Those steps would come in a whirlwind, a whirlwind in which two became one, a whirlwind in which Cecil and I were "co-missioned."

Called Together

After Cecil and I were married and serving at Woodlawn Christian Church in Campbellsville, Kentucky, I began praying that we would win the Reader's Digest Sweepstakes so that we could leave our ministry in Kentucky and go to the mission field. It didn't happen. We were, however, called to take another step.

At the same time that I was praying about winning the Reader's Digest Sweepstakes, Cecil had asked the body at Woodlawn to pray that God would raise up someone from within the congregation to go to the uttermost parts of the world and preach the Gospel.

God answered that prayer. He raised up us!

God sent Al Hamilton, who was launching Pioneer Bible Translators, to speak at Woodlawn Christian Church. By the end of Al's visit (he was spending the weekend with us), Cecil and I were the first recruits for this new venture. Woodlawn was not so happy, but Al was delirious.

Two weeks later, we set off for Norman, Oklahoma, to begin linguistics training with the Summer Institute of Linguistics, hoping to be trained as Bible translators for the new field Pioneer Bible Translators wanted to open in Papua New Guinea. We drove into Norman, Oklahoma, in the midst of a tornado, pulling a little U-Haul trailer loaded with all of our earthly possessions – a toy box and a baby crib. Sirens were blaring; leaves, dust, and debris were whirling everywhere. We had to pull over on the side of the road and wait it out. I don't know why we weren't killed. I guess the eye of the tornado missed us, but there was no visibility whatsoever. We waited that out and then continued on to the school. We checked into our one dorm room with bathrooms down the hall. Thankfully, we could squeeze the crib and toy box between our desks and bed so that we could keep our baby! We didn't want to give him up just because we were expecting another.

At that point, we didn't know how we would live, but we did have a month's salary in hand and a few hundred dollars from a money tree the church had given us. That was sufficient for our room and board and tuition for the three months in Norman. We made it through the summer with our heads full of phonetics, phonology, grammar, and literacy, and then set out for nine more months of advanced training in Dallas at the International Linguistics Center.

Cecil was able to work at the school to pay our bill there. By then, I was seven

months pregnant with our second child and in need of a doctor. I, along with four other prospective missionary wives at the International Linguistics Center, became the patients of a doctor who was sympathetic to Wycliffe Bible Translators. We had no health insurance, but the Methodist Hospital in Dallas waived the pre-admittance payment and allowed us to pay for our baby's delivery and hospital on a monthly payment plan.

Cecil began an interim weekend ministry at Bella Vista Christian Church in Garland, Texas, just outside of Dallas. The salary he received from this ministry was a great help in paying the hospital bill in the coming months. He continued to minister at Bella Vista until we finished our training in May. The Bella Vista church continued to support us after we left Dallas, becoming one of our first supporters in missions work. Even though, several years later, the church closed its doors, two dear couples from that church have continued to support the Byrd family to this very day.

During our second semester at Dallas, Cecil determined that his desire was to minister overseas by preaching and teaching the Word rather than by translating it. He resumed talks with Dean Davis (we had first talked to Dean during our senior year at Johnson Bible College) concerning church planting and leadership training in Zambia. By May, 1975, we were accepted by Zambia Christian Mission as missionary recruits to Ndola, Zambia. We left Dallas and returned to Kentucky to raise support to go to Zambia.

Raising Support

If going is the hardest aspect of being obedient to the Great Commission, then raising support is often the aspect that blocks the obedience. Before I ever was a missionary, I desired every part of being a missionary except that part that involved raising support. Even though I had never attempted it (except for a summer's internship in Grande Prairie, Alberta, Canada), I knew that I wouldn't like it. Raising support seemed an impossible task to accomplish.

When the year of training at the Summer Institute of Linguistics in Norman, Oklahoma, and the International Linguistics Center in Dallas, TX, finished in May, 1975, we headed back to Campbellsville, KY. We started out living with an area minister and his family -- the four of us (Cecil, Ben, Miriam, and I) in

the older daughter's bedroom. By the end of the summer, we had moved into our own apartment. My former college roommate's mother lived across the street from us, and a very nice older couple lived beside us.

From that low-income apartment in Campbellsville, we sent out one hundred letters telling about our desire to go as missionaries to Zambia.

From those letters, we received five responses. These responses led to speaking engagements, which led to other speaking engagements and to more speaking engagements. In order to provide for the family during the early support-raising days, Cecil worked part-time for Campbellsville Industries (a company that made steeples for church buildings) and filled the pulpit at area churches when he was not on the road raising support. When people would come to the low income housing project looking for someone who could clean their houses, I'd drag my two little children and go with them, not so much that I needed the money, but more because I couldn't tell these old people no. The housing project was not the greatest place to live, but at least it was our own place. I can still see the linoleum floors of the apartment and the sparse furniture that people had loaned to us.

During the support-raising trips, Cecil often preached from one of his favorite passages of Scripture, Ephesians 2:1-10. He was so drawn to that passage because it clearly described what God had done for him – once dead in sin and now alive in Christ.

There are so many memories from those trips, like being in Jefferson City, Missouri, when we received word that Cecil's brother, Leon, had been killed in Virginia; Miriam choking on a potato chip at the home we were visiting; weeklong stays in places like Flat Rock, Indiana, for VBS and a camp in Kansas; and finally, having to remain behind in Campbellsville with two small children when the traveling got to be too much for all of us with endless hours in the car, unbalanced meals, and late nights driving with no place to lay our heads. It was hard being separated when it wasn't possible for the whole family to travel. I counted on Cecil to administer discipline in the household. Once when he was away, Ben squirted a man who was painting the water hydrant with his water

gun. The man was NOT happy. I so wished for Cecil's presence when I learned what had happened. Cecil also found it difficult to be away from us. That long three-week trip Cecil made to Texas alone was way too long to be apart, and he vowed never to let that happen again. He never did. That three-week separation was the longest we ever endured.

After 18 months and thousands of miles traveled, God provided for our first-time expenses and $1,200 in committed monthly support through 30 churches,

Sunday school classes, and individuals. By God's grace, our support was raised! And then, almost seven years into our marriage, we were ready to go together to the land to which God had "co-missioned" us.

Shipping

We were advised by missionaries in Zambia to ship any and everything we thought we would need to furnish a house and live in Zambia. God provided for these needs through the Swinford family in Flat Rock, Indiana.

Mr. Swinford took us to Belknap in Louisville, Kentucky, and we picked out everything we needed -- appliances, transformers, beds, living room furniture, end tables, dressers, and a chest of drawers. Then Mr. Swinford invited Cecil and Ben to come to Flat Rock to his lumberyard to build the crates for shipping these items. The crates were built and packed in that lumberyard and loaded onto a farm truck which Cecil, accompanied by four-year-old Ben, drove to the shipping docks in New York. I guess you might call us do-it-yourself missionaries.

The crates arrived in Ndola, Zambia, where they were stored to wait our arrival. We needed to get to Ndola quickly. Dean and Judy Davis and Charlie and Betty Delaney were moving to Lusaka and needed us to move into one of the houses and oversee the Ndola work.

Support was raised; crates were shipped; it was time to go.

Ye

Big C, Me, and We

Cecil Curtis Byrd

At Johnson Bible College, the guys on campus called him "Big C." I'm not sure why. Was it because he was over 6 feet tall and a very good basketball player? Was it because he was seven years older than the average freshman in the college? I don't know why they started calling him "Big C," but "Big C" was who he was on campus.

Big C's parents, Wilmer Curtis Byrd and Mabel Eloise Elkins Byrd, named him Cecil Curtis Byrd on October 6, 1943, the day Mabel Eloise gave birth to him in Huntington, West Virginia. Wilmer Curtis and Mabel Eloise were both very young when Cecil was born. They took him home from the hospital in Huntington to live in the coal-mining town of Welch in McDowell Country, West Virginia. Two years later, Cecil's brother, Leon, was born; and two years after that, their brother, Danny, joined them. Two more years passed, and their brother, Walton, came into the world; and in--you guessed it-- two more years, the Byrd boys welcomed a baby sister, Sharon, into the family.

What followed was a rough and rowdy childhood. Cecil's mother was known to be a kind and good-hearted person, often ministering to the needs of other people. Cecil remembered the times his mom would fix the neighborhood ladies' hair for them on Saturday afternoons. Cecil seemed to have inherited the heart of his mother. In the years that I knew him, he loved to help people. He was never too busy to lend someone a hand, help out those

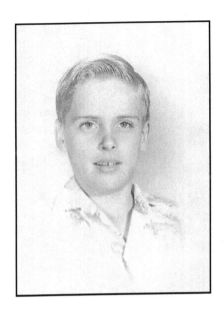

in need, give the shirt off his back or the dishes out of our kitchen cabinets to those who lacked any such things.

One of Cecil's favorite memories of his growing up years was hunting for a Christmas tree in this forested area of West Virginia. The family brought the tree home to their little house that was carved into the side of a mountain and decorated it on Christmas Eve. On Christmas morning, Cecil and his brothers and sister would rush to the tree to find brown paper sacks filled with nuts, hard Christmas candies, and candied orange slices.

As Cecil grew up, swinging on a rope across a cavern was a favorite pastime. The day came, however, when the rope broke. Not only did the rope break, but, when it fell to the bottom of the cavern, so did both of Cecil's

arms. With both of his arms broken, Cecil was back to being fed by his mom. That was no fun for an 11-year-old boy.

Around the age of 14, adolescence took over Cecil's life. He slicked back his hair in the fashion of the day and rolled up his t-shirt sleeves. Think of Fonzie on "Happy Days." Now you've got the picture!

Cecil remembered the times his mother would take him along to church at the community Church of God. The red-headed preacher could preach a loud and fiery sermon; but for some reason, that preacher's sermons didn't make an immediate difference in Cecil's life. Instead, his feet were traveling the wide road, a road that led to the Washington, D.C. Reformatory for Boys. At the age of 14, Cecil developed the habit of stealing money from the U.S. mail. That habit cost him some time in the reformatory. I don't think it reformed him, though. He got out, but he wasn't reformed.

Cecil's dad was a coal-miner who left early each morning with his lunch bucket in hand. Cecil and his three brothers and sister got in big trouble if they took the last of the Little Debbie oatmeal cakes and Swiss rolls that were purchased for that lunch bucket. All five of them got whippings until the guilty party confessed.

On Saturdays, Cecil's dad liked to get together with some of the other musically-inclined coalminers to churn out a little Bluegrass music. Curtis played a mean harmonica. The children loved to hear him make that harmonica sound like a train whistle.

The music sessions were accompanied by indulgence in alcohol. That boded ill for the family, both for Mabel and for the children. Alcohol made Curtis mean, and his family often bore the brunt of it. Cecil particularly remembered the night his dad, in a fit of anger, said, "You think I can't pick this table up and throw it out the door?" The children were sure that he could and that he very well might.

When Cecil turned his life over to God, a chief desire in his heart was that his dad would do the same. Every visit to his dad's home included a plea for him to give his life to Christ. In 1998, not long before his death, Curtis accepted Christ as his Savior and was baptized. Cecil, along with the angels in Heaven, rejoiced.

After a long stint of coalmining, the Byrd family moved to Spencer, Virginia, where Cecil's dad worked at a saw mill. Cecil's mom worked as a nursing assistant in a nearby hospital. Being the oldest child, Cecil had the responsibility for the care of his brothers and sister when his mother was working or sleeping days in order to work nights. He cooked for them and ironed their clothes. Because his mother worked the night shift, it was Cecil's responsibility to make sure his brothers and sister were ready to catch the school bus each morning.

On December 14, 1960, the children missed the school bus. Their mother got home in time to load them in her car to take them to school. As they were driving down the hill, Mabel told the children, "One day we're going to fix up this old Lizzie and take a trip back to West Virginia."

About that time, the tires hit a patch of ice and the car slammed into the side of the hill. Mabel's head was severed from her body.

For years and years afterward, Cecil blamed himself for his mother's death. In his mind, if he had made sure that he and his three brothers and sister had

caught the school bus that morning, his mother would not have died. It was not until 10 years later, when Cecil understood God's sovereignty, that he was able to find release from this burden of guilt.

In the meantime, however, the cycle of sin which had begun in his early teen-aged years worsened. At the age of 17, Cecil was spiraling down a path of destruction. Theft, breaking and entering, car theft, and other convictions led to time in the county jail, parole under Bro. Rockwell's supervision, breaking rock at a work farm in Bluefield, incarceration in Louisiana--the list goes on. Some in the small community in which he lived attributed this downward spiral along a rocky road to the traumatic loss of his mother.

After his final stint with the law, Cecil made his way to California to seek his fortune in Hollywood. He aspired to be a movie star but ended up teaching three-year-olds in a Montessori school in Santa Monica. During the day, he taught school in Santa Monica, and during the evenings he attended classes at East Los Angeles University, and most nights he partied--until the day he was convicted that his life must change, and he returned to Virginia to pursue a new life in Christ.

Cecil did not like to talk about those days in which he was so far from God except to testify that, by God's grace, he was no longer that man--he was a new creature in Christ. That is why, during our 18 months of support-raising, he frequently preached this passage of Scripture from Ephesians 2:1-10 (NIV):

> As for you, you were dead in your transgressions and sins, in which you used to live when you followed the ways of this world and of the ruler of the kingdom of the air, the spirit who is now at work in those who are disobedient. All of us also lived among them at one time, gratifying the cravings of our sinful nature and following its desires and thoughts. Like the rest, we were by na-

ture objects of wrath. But because of his great love for us, God, who is rich in mercy, made us alive with Christ even when we were dead in transgressions—it is by grace you have been saved. And God raised us up with Christ and seated us with him in the heavenly realms in Christ Jesus, in order that in the coming ages he might show the incomparable riches of his grace, expressed in his kindness to us in Christ Jesus. For it is by grace you have been saved, through faith—and this not from yourselves, it is the gift of God— not by works, so that no one can boast. For we are God's workmanship, created in Christ Jesus to do good works, which God prepared in advance for us to do.

This passage so accurately described Cecil's old self and what happened to it. He was so happy to be rid of that life. His love for God and gratitude to God was magnified because he knew from whence he had come, and he never wanted to go back to that life filled with sin.

There were at least a couple of students from Martinsville, Virginia, at Johnson Bible College. Milford was a sheriff's son. He filled me in on some of the escapades from Cecil's former life. I didn't listen with my mind. Love is blind and deaf.

Sandy had known Cecil through her brother. She said that she would never have known that the person at Johnson Bible College was the same guy that ran around with her brother. His speech was different; his manner was different; his actions were different. He was a new creature. Now that's what I wanted to hear. I only wanted to know the new creature. The old was in the past.

For a long time, I didn't know that Cecil had four tattoos, two on each arm, just above and below the bend of each elbow. They were the nicknames of his three cohorts and himself: Joke, Red, Byrd, and Alki. From the time he stepped on the campus of Johnson Bible College in August, 1968, Cecil wore long-sleeved shirts to cover those tattoos. He was ashamed. They reminded him of his former life. Then basketball season started. You can't play basketball in a long-sleeved shirt. He showed me the tattoos. He was still ashamed. I didn't care. They were of his former life. God had made him a new creature. To me, they were left as a testimony of God's redeeming power in the life of the man I loved.

Soon after we were married, during one of our trips to Virginia, Cecil introduced me to Alki. Alki was the son of a preacher. He had taken a different path from his dad. But, praise God, he came back to God.

When Cecil took me to Alki's trailer, Alki and his wife were in mourning. Their baby had died. They showed me the pictures of their precious baby in her little casket. It was heart-breaking. But Alki and his wife had God as their Comforter. Praise God for the redeeming blood of Jesus that covers all sin and bridges the gap between sinful man and God. Praise God for the blood of Jesus that washes away all sin and makes us whiter than snow.

Now let me tell you about this new creature, Cecil Byrd. He was very compassionate toward people and very open. Once he was over the shame of his past life, he was open and friendly to most everyone. We often had people over to our house, and Cecil was the one who entertained them. He was a good

26

husband and a great father. He loved giving gifts, even when he couldn't afford to buy them. He spent money on faith, and I kept the checkbook.

The children loved him dearly. He was a strict disciplinarian, but he also was loving and lots of fun. Although he could be consumed by and with his work, he would make time to take the boys fishing (and sometimes the girls, too) on week-long fishing trips. Sometimes on Saturday mornings, he would make his special West Virginia pancakes: water, flour, and baking powder mixed to the proper consistency and poured into a greased cast-iron skillet.

Every pancake was the size of the skillet. He would call the children to the table one at a time so that each pancake would be served piping hot. They would cover them with peanut butter and syrup. They all loved their dad's special pancakes. Sometimes we would team up for another Saturday morning treat: I would make biscuits and he would make the best-ever gravy. Saturday mornings were fun.

Sometimes on Sunday nights, Cecil would make a batch of fudge. He made it the old-fashioned way by boiling it to the soft-ball stage and adding peanut butter as the last ingredient. After he poured the fudge onto greased plates, he would give each of the children a spoon so that they could scrape the pot and lick the spoon.

Here's the recipe:
  9 tbs. of cocoa
  1 c of milk
  3 c of sugar
  1 dash of salt
  1.5 tsp. of vanilla
  peanut butter
  nuts (optional)

Under low heat, allow the cocoa to thoroughly mix with the milk. Add sugar, mix thoroughly, increase heat, and stir continuously until the mixture boils to prevent sticking to the sides or bottom of the pan. Put a small amount of tap water in a teacup. Place a tbsp. of the mixture in the water. Can you form a ball with it? If so, remove from heat. If not, allow the mixture to continue boiling, repeating the water test until you have the soft ball consistency. Remove from heat. Add vanilla. Do not stir. Add 3 heaping tbsp. of peanut butter, either crunchy or smooth. If you use smooth, you can add other nuts if desired.

Do not stir. Butter two dinner plate. Allow mixture to sit and cool a bit. When cool, stir rather briskly and quickly. Pour immediately onto the plates before the mixture hardens. Allow to cool. Then cut into squares and chill in fridge.

Cecil was not much of a letter-writer, so his letters, when written, were true expressions of love. Here's one he wrote to Ben, Miriam, Kathy, and the grandchildren while he, Daniel, Deborah, and I were in Mozambique:

"First of all, I love you so much. Then you must know that I seldom ever miss a day praying for our Lord's blessings upon you. May you be faithful to him in all things. We are keeping extremely busy here. These people are poor, hungry, sick, and dying, constantly in need of something. I know you'll remember how it is. I pray that we might have wisdom in knowing how to minister to them. We depend on our Father to provide the necessary strength and guidance one day at a time. Today Mom took Daniel and Deborah swimming at one of the clubs in town. No school because it was a holiday. I'm sure they enjoyed it. Mom left here with their faces as white as a sheet after rubbing on the sunscreen. Daniel is having great fun with his soccer team. They are in a tourney with ten teams. Daniel and team tied their first game, 0-0. You should hear Daniel tell it, 'They are like glue on me, Dad. They know to get me.' Ben, I think of you working in the cold and snow. Hope you are keeping warm. Miriam, hope you are still happy with your work. Tell Joanna how much we miss her. We have lots of her pictures, (Joanna is our first grand-daughter), and Mom says she is going to put up more. Kathy, you are still smiling from your picture at me when I step out of our bedroom. Hope you get to come in May and have lots of time to smile in person. Ben, give Leah hugs and kisses for me. (Leah is our second granddaughter.) Have her picture on the wall too. Kathy and Miriam said y'alls house is very nice. Our Lord is good to us, isn't he? We are slowly adding wardrobes and chests of drawers. Only Mom needs a wardrobe now. And we hope to bring it back this weekend from South Africa. Kathy, I don't see the Little Debbies yet, but M&Ms are around and also Snickers. We still get good bread, and there is a person here at the center selling Cokes. But not to worry, you know Dad has complete control over sweets. Ben, I'm going to a friend's to tape the UK and U of L basketball game and also the Super Bowl. Miriam, hope you got your car winterized, because I heard of it snowing in Tennessee and Ohio. Louisville will soon get it. And Kathy, you're all set? Temperatures today were over 100 degrees. Heard it said that the chicken farmers were finding hard-boiled eggs in the hen-houses. Now, I ain't got no proof of that, you understand. Well now, my children, you all write us a letter, mail them to Ron and Bev's, and they will email them on to us. This whole procedure could take less than three days! Love to hear how things are going with each one of you. Greet the church for us. Going to close for now. Mimi, Happy Birthday! Love you girl. Love you Ben. Love you Kathy. Love you Joanna. Love you Leah. All for now."

Today as the wind was whipping and howling outside, I was reminded of April 3, 1974, when tornadoes whipped through Taylor County and Adair Country, destroying everything in their paths. I remember finishing supper at the kitchen table when we heard a roar in the distance behind our house. We ran to the back door to see why a freight train would be passing so close to the house. As we looked, we could see in the distance a funnel cloud moving. While watching, Cecil got a call from the rescue squad and, being a faithful member, he took Baby Ben and me down to the unfinished, cold, concrete-floored, damp-walled basement of the parsonage in which we were living in Campbellsville, Kentucky. Equipping us with the playpen for Ben to sleep in and a quilt for me to lie on and a rocking chair to rock in, he said, "Don't leave this basement until I come back." I obeyed my husband and ended up spending the whole night in the basement, not knowing what was going on up above while he was out rescuing the broken world of Taylor County, Kentucky.

That's pretty much who Cecil was – a man who secured his family and went out to save the world.

So here's my summary: Cecil Curtis Byrd, "Big C," redeemed by the blood of the Lamb, made new in Christ so he could pass on the Love of Jesus to others.

Tributes from His Sons

The following reflections from Ben and Daniel bring a sense of clarity to the kind of man Cecil was in the eyes of his sons:

Cecil
By Benjamin Curtis Byrd

On the back of a Mattress Warehouse invoice, I found these notes written about Cecil by his firstborn son, Ben, during the days we were waiting in Kentucky for Cecil's dead body to arrive from Mozambique:

The preacher in Cecil...his passion was to spread the message of Christ through God's Word .
The teacher in Cecil......his desire was to teach the Gospel to believers.
The evangelist in Cecil....his priority was to win others to Christ.
The father in Cecil.....love of his own kids.
The dad in Cecil.....dedication to each individual child's needs.
The fun dad....many, many fishing trips, each eventful in its own way.
The teacher dad...often iterated points about life which can't be iterated enough.
The discipline dad....the long, stone-faced discussions, usually before a paddling, that made the child understand the wrong he had done despite anticipation of "the paddle."
The hungry dad.....biscuits and gravy, Little Debbie oatmeal pies, Whoppers, Fig Newtons, fried eggs and bacon.
The when-you're-in-a-hurry-and-slows-you-down dad....popping the hood on your vehicle to check oil and fluids because he cares and has no concept of the time constraint you're under!

A Great Man
By Daniel Wells Byrd

My father was a great man. There have been many, many great men in history. People are considered great for various reasons and certainly there are levels of greatness. What makes a person great in the eyes of one individual may not hold the same weight in the estimation of another. This relativity therefore, most definitely makes defining greatness an elusive task. Some would say it is purely a subjective determination. I believe there must be some universal themes to greatness. Something else to consider when talking about greatness is the idea that people are, in a sense, transcendent and beyond definition. There are always thought processes, deep heart ruminations, and internal desires that are invisible and unknowable to others. People are complex. Therefore, defining them is risky. With this in mind, when I say that he was a great man, I am not saying everything about him was great. Rather when I call him great I am referring to the many good qualities I perceived him to have had that superseded and outweighed his fewer misgiving characteristics. The colors of his nature which painted a portrait of greatness were: his noble character, compassionate, generous, self-sacrificial, hardworking, fun loving, enthusiastic, positive, humorous, athletic, good looking, kind, intelligent, well-known, distinguished, down to earth, gentle, compelling, genuine, honest, reliable, grateful, decisive, fearless, adventurous, spontaneous, faithful, and confident to name a few.

However, I fear these adjectives simply scratch the surface when attempting to get to the bottom of just why he was great. Perhaps graduating to one-liners will better serve the cause. He had an ease about him that made people comfortable. He would give you the shirt off his back, the plates in his cupboard, and the money in his pocket. There's no one he didn't have time for. There was little he would stop short of in order to help a stranger. His smile was disarming and his laugh was contagious. He joked in a way that reeked of joy. He had a way with words and knew just what to say and how to say it to meet people's needs. He carried himself with a "God is for me" kind of posture. You could sense the goodness of his heart through the tone of his voice. There was an aura of determination you could sense that spoke of his desire to make a difference. He had a stubborn refusal built into him to not waver from his values, his beliefs, or his mission. It was obvious he had been deeply touched by God. He was a driven man, a man driven by love; love for God, love for family, and love for the marginalized, the forgotten, and the oppressed.

But I fear this still does not do justice when describing his greatness. Short of knowing someone personally and intimately, I believe greatness is best captured within the context of story. His life, in my young, adoring eyes, seemed larger in size than other lives. His work seemed of greater importance and significance compared to other trades. People treated him as if he was powerful and influential. They welcomed him in their homes, in their villages, and into their lives. As a boy, he took me with him on his travels, not only across North America on his fund raising trips to churches where we stayed in the homes of church members and fished in their ponds and lakes but also on his preaching tours in the bush of Africa where we slept in tents and fished in rivers. He was always on the move. As the Zambians described him, "he was strong and moved in the night."

Here I will only manage to piece some parts of his life together and merely frame a pale, fragmented picture of his actual life which was a triumphant

31

story that moves from tragedy, to transformation, to redemption even in the face of more tragedy. But the story of his life is not the central purpose of this writing. A stronger thread I want to weave into this tapestry is how his life was formative for my own and how I have come to be my own man having grown up under his leadership and journeying through various stages of grief and thought after his murder.

There was a time shortly after his death I probably esteemed him just a little lower than the gods, so to speak. I suppose a lot of that elevation was a coping mechanism I employed to deal with his untimely and senseless death. Although less venerated now, he remains a hero of mine. There was period of time I wanted to be him, I think in some ways in order to keep him alive and present still. I wore his clothes and colognes, imitated his gestures, attempted to sound like him, went to the same college as him, pursued the same degree and went into full-time Christian ministry just like him. I visited his friends to hear them tell stories about him. I became quite obsessed with him.

Before I go any further, it should be said that in all reality by no means do I currently believe he was without fault. He had many imperfections and shortcomings which were in plain sight on many an occasion. I'm aware there is a tendency to exaggerate, glamorize and embellish the life of the deceased, especially when they are admired and missed by their loved ones. A telling of his life from the perspective of a still grieving son who has always loved and idolized his father even before he was brutally murdered in front him, could easily come across as distorted and less than accurate. I realize this and it is not my intention to misconstrue reality for the sake of his honor or reputation. He was in all actuality, a great man not simply because he was murdered but because of the life he lived for the sake of others.

He grew up in the impoverished hills of West Virginia where his father, Curtis, worked as a meager waged coal miner. He relied on the bottle to dull the effects of his arduous and less than rewarding lifestyle and took his remaining frustrations out on his wife and children. My father's mother, Mabel Eloise, worked hard as a third shift nurse to try and make ends meet. There were four boys and one girl in the family. Since my grandmother was not there in the mornings to wake, cook breakfast, pack lunches, and get the children ready, this responsibility fell to my father who was the oldest of the siblings.

On one cold and icy winter morning, my father hadn't managed to get the kids out the door in time to meet the school bus. When my grandmother got home, an argument ensued between her and Curtis who was leaving for work. She drove the children teary eyed to school but tragically on the way hit some ice, slid up onto a hillside and rolled the car. The car landed on Eloise's head and she died instantly. None of the kids were hurt. My father was 14 at the time. He felt the accident was his fault. He blamed himself for her death. Had he just gotten the kids to the bus stop all would have been avoided. It took him ten years to come to terms that he was not responsible. He fell into a life of crime in the years that followed. He was in and out of juvenile correction farms, jails, and state prisons. He developed a reputation as a fearless fighter who never backed down from a brawl. During one of his stays in prison, a preacher reached him with the gospel of Jesus Christ and soon he was released on house arrest under the care of a Baptist minister. After a period of good behavior, my dad decided to make a go of it in Hollywood as an actor but made it only as far as teaching at a Montessori school. It was there he decided that if he was going to live the Christian life he was going to have to become a minister. Ministry was to help keep him accountable so the story goes.

He was man of extremes, I reckon. When Robert Kennedy was shot and killed, he was spurred to trek back across the country and enroll in Johnson Bible College, a small Christian college in Knoxville, Tennessee. He smoked his last cigarette before being dropped off at the college campus where he showed up with 11 dollars in his pocket. This was consistent with the college's mantra which is: Open day and night to the poor young man who desires above every other desire to preach the gospel of Jesus Christ. He worked his way through college as a farm hand. He met my mother there and they were married on campus. They answered the call to become missionaries to Africa in the early 1970s. The rest, as they say, is history. The stories my mother tells about their early adventures in Zambia could fill a book. In fact she is writing a book much to the delight of our family. She has a memory like a steel trap.

I was born during their service in Zambia. Dad planted 16 churches in Zambia. He spent his days teaching and equipping the Zambian men to lead their churches and helping the families of the congregations in all areas of their lives. Mom primarily was a homemaker in Zambia. When we moved to neighboring Mozambique she taught first grade at the primary school where I attended. It was all during this time that I closely watched my father and was enamored by his work. I was fortunate to go to many places in Africa and the U.S. I had the privilege of meeting and eating with hundreds of people. He loved fishing. So I got to experience many great fishing holes. I saw the best and the worst of my father as he passionately carried out his work. His anger surfaced and spewed when one thing after another wouldn't go right. I saw him openly praise God with his signature, "Thank ya Lord," when things would in fact turn out right. I saw him diligently study and prepare for his sermons and watch videos and write papers for his master's degree in New Testament. I would peruse his library and examine his highlights and notes that he would make in his books. He would stay up late and throw darts with me and watch action movies with me. He supported my desire to play sports and attended many soccer matches. He helped me and the villagers carve out a soccer field for our community and was genuinely interested in and even assisted in my overall enjoyment of life. He was a friend and a mentor. We shared a close relationship.

In terms of my spiritual development, my father was always very instrumental before and even after his death. When I was a child he would read the Bible and other Christian stories to me before bed. I can remember his prayers after reading ending regularly in, "….and give him a long, long life to live and many, many years to serve you, Lord. And keep the evil one far away from him." He would lead the family in family devotions in the evenings and ask one of us to pray at the dinner table. We were in church every Sunday and most Wednesdays. I asked him if he would baptize me when I was 11 years old. I told him I understood that Jesus died for my sins and I wanted to make him my savior and Lord. I can remember being so excited about my decision and I read my little red NIV hardcover Bible my parents gave me every night before bed and I prayed regularly. I personally wanted to be a good Christian not just to make my dad proud but because I genuinely believed and wanted to please God. I remember going with him to Christian camps when he was the featured missionary for the week. I wanted to share stories about Africa as well and I wanted to do my part to support the ministry. In Mozambique, he built be a wooden sheath for my Bible that he fastened to my bedside wall. That way I could pull my "Sword of the Spirit" out of its sheath to read it. He printed out 1 Tim 4:12 which reads,"don't let anyone look down on you because you are young but set an example for the believers in speech, conduct, love and purity" and taped it to my door. I began reaching out to my young African friends giving them clothes and throwing parties during holidays--serving them bread with peanut butter and jam and coke. I started a soccer team and asked for uniforms and other gear to be sent from the States so I could pass that out to my friends in the community who had nothing. I became active in my school's Christian youth group. I wanted to be serve God because I felt the desire in my heart but also because Dad was my example and he was watching me. He would always tell me to remember who I was when leaving on dates or going to school parties. Watching him throughout my adolescence help other people definitely helped shape my own servant's heart and my desire to live generously and compassionately.

It's often been said you first learn what God is like through your parents. This was especially true for me given the fact my dad was a minister – one whose paid profession is to speak and act on behalf of God. I took a sys-tematic theology course during my undergrad. I learned about God's nature, his transcendence, his holiness, his goodness, wisdom, infiniteness, oneness, wrath, sovereignty, omnipotence, omniscience etc. I loved studying about it and still do because it interests me. Perhaps the greatest attribute of God that I learned from Dad on a practical and experiential level was God's imminence. Dad understood that God is near us, within us, and among us. He emphasized and pointed out that God is active in the world and interested in the minutia of our lives. It was like God was walking beside him every step of the way. He talked with him out loud, he sung praises in the car and in the shower, he prayed openly in public frequently. If an ambulance passed by on the road he would say, "bless them Lord." If there was a near miss in a traffic incident he would say, "thank you Father." When people asked what his plans were he would say, "Lord willing, I will do this." He brought God to bear on every-thing that was going on around him. This is why when he was killed I was so heartbroken. In my mind at the time, it was as if God had betrayed this man who walked so closely and intimately with him. What happened to the protection I thought our family was entitled to from serving God? We always had seemed to be delivered from other threats and dangers. My greatest question became if God is near us and with us and he was there that night, why on earth would he have allowed such a horrible thing?

I suppressed those angry thoughts and instead chose to praise and serve God publically as minister and missionary like my father had done, while inwardly I blamed God for abandoning us and doubted his goodness. After more trials, struggles and disappointments which directly arose out of missionary work, I soon resented the idea of God's imminence and shrugged God completely out of my life. Which, in retrospect, was of no consolation. In fact, it caused way more grief and sadness. Nevertheless, I wanted to go my own way. I began seriously analyzing my motives for taking up ministry and even regretted that I had pursued the Bible College route to begin with. It became clear that when I first began pursuing Christian ministry and studying theology, it was as if I was bargaining with God. If I became a pastor then God would absolve the guilt I felt surrounding Dad's death. Secondly, I was hoping to gain Dad's approval or at least the personal satisfaction of fulfilling my father's wishes for me to become a minister. The only way I could be happy was if I carried on my dad's work. If I didn't God wouldn't bless me, so I reasoned, because it would be selfish for me to pursue my own desires.

What's changed? Who am I today and what, if anything, would I have done differently? The short answers are: I think differently about God. I don't blame him for my dad's death and don't believe he abandoned us. I personally am a lover of God and believe in his goodness and goodwill towards us. I believe he wants good things for us. Part of my identity is that I am a seeker who wants to pursue a deeper relationship with God. I love life and people. I have an enthusiasm to live life wide open. I am not someone who will be restricted by legalism and judgment and lifeless religious tradition. I want to know the living God who celebrates life on earth and delights in his creation. I am a servant of God and want to do the work of putting his world back together through the passions and talents God has instilled in me innately and through my experiences and influences, not the least of which was my father. Had I not entered into ministry preparation I would have never learned the lessons of God that I now cling to. Like how God is good and loves me no matter if I am a straight edged minister or rough around the edges construction worker. And had I not ignored God, perhaps I wouldn't have realized that there is not some magic protective force field surrounding those who walk with God on this earth. There is no promise of physical safety even though God is with us and near to us. The only real answer to the ever real and present danger of this world is Jesus and his triumph over death. It is normal to undergo the negative effects of the world. Even Jesus experienced that and called God into question. What I have come to truly believe and cling to is simply in God's goodness and his wisdom in creating the world. I trust that what we can have with him in this life and the life to come is far greater than trials we experience on earth. So today, looking back, I don't think I would have done anything differently. I believe God is with me and is guiding me even when I don't make the best possible decisions or when the systems in place in the world collide and I reap the ill effects. I do believe, however, that he can make good out of bad and redeem the mess we make out of our own lives. I believe that is the supernatural providence and wisdom of God that is beyond our comprehension.

Whether my dad was never a missionary and regardless if he had never died the way he did, living the way of Jesus, the way of love is the best possible way to live. Selflessness is more fulfilling and rewarding than selfishness. Generosity is more enjoyable than being stingy. Mercy and forgiveness are healthier than hate and vengeance. Acceptance is more life-giving and freeing than judgment. Praising others is good for the soul while criticism makes you bitter. I simply believe that Christian character and a life patterned after the teachings of Jesus is more beneficial, enjoyable and enriching than one that is centered around purely human philosophies. I am grateful for the father I had and for the time we had to spend together. He indelibly shaped my life. However, I have made my own decisions and have become my own man. And I believe he would be proud of that. My aim is to now make God proud by being me and delving deeper into a relationship with him that is honest, genuine, and authentic.

The Beggar
By Daniel Wells Byrd

He steered his pick-up truck around a beggar lying naked in the middle of the road, apparently unconscious, just outside the school grounds where I attended high school in Maputo, Mozambique Africa. He pulled his pickup truck up to the gate and waited for the guard to come and open it like usual. It was Friday and he had come to pick me, my mother and my two sisters up from school. He was in a hurry because we were going to South Africa for the weekend and had to get to the border before it closed at 6pm and the roads were in bad shape. He was already cutting it close time wise and you never knew what the border traffic was going to be like. As he waited, he watched vehicles narrowly missing the beggar who was now rolling around in the street. Homeless beggars were a common sight in the city. They were either strung out on drugs or close to incoherently drunk. Some of them were also mentally ill and wandered the streets singing or mumbling insensibilities as they asked for money. They rarely bathed and reeked of the most rancid stench imaginable from defecating and urinating on themselves. The inept and corrupt government did not have the services to care for them and most of the general public simply ignored them.

The beggar was in plain view of my classmates waiting for their parents to pick them up. Some of them laughed and pointed and one even threw something at him in jest. It was understood no one was about to do anything about it. My dad took this all in as he waited at the gate and watched. My dad was not the kind of person who could stand by. He was generally the person who stopped to help people broken down on the side of road, intervened if there

36

was a shouting match between people in public, picked up hitch hikers, etc. After pulling his truck into the school parking lot, he said "Daniel come with me." He walked confidently, briskly, and determinedly into the middle of the road while gesturing for traffic to stop. Everyone stopped what they doing and directed their attention toward what was unfolding in disbelief. A well-to-do white man, showing concern for the least valued in an impoverished African country, even dirtying his hands for the sake of this man's wellbeing.

I reluctantly walked behind him, my head down, heavy with embarrassment. I was 14 at the time and was far more concerned with what my friends thought and with being cool than with helping right the world's wrongs. It seemed like such a long walk, almost like trudging through quicksand, to get to the beggar. I resolved to fix my gaze on my dad to ignore all the eyes I felt were groping me. I remember looking deeply at him or maybe into him and discerning a complex combination of emotions stirring within him. I saw these emotions surface many times on separate occasions. But for some reason, I remember an emotional convergence during this particular scenario. I think he was frustrated at the indifference of the onlookers. I think he felt sorry for the beggar. I think he sympathized with the beggar's pain and was moved with compassion to help. I think there was righteous anger regarding the ever present cruelty and injustice in the world. I think there was some futile desperation in there as well. He knew picking this man up and moving him to the sidewalk would only temporarily help the man's problems. I also saw some of his perpetual life angst come out that day. In his eyes there was always someone needing help and not enough time and resources to do it.

As he reached under the man's armpits the man vomited a little and my dad turned his head. I gagged a little at the man's stench and dropped his feet. Dad got a little impatient at this point and told me to "come on son." I couldn't help but look at the man's genitals and the bumps that were on him. His hair was filthy and he had open sores on his abdomen and legs. We carried him to the side and laid him there out of the flow of traffic as the world literally stood still and watched. We walked back over to the truck and as we drove away I looked back and the man had rolled back into the street. I remember Dad saying, "sometimes you can only do so much." Was he disappointed that the man rolled back into the street? Yes. Yet he had some satisfaction from at least attempting something positive. He used to say "the work is never done." To Cecil Byrd, the reward was doing the right thing. That was the kind of man my dad was. He was missionary. He was a servant. This was his identity.

Tributes from His Friends

"For This Love"

Martin Sanders, missionary to Colombia, wrote the following words in honor of Cecil, set them to music, and sang them with Jeff and Monica Fife at Johnson Bible College Homecoming, 2000, a month after Cecil's death:

There's no place he will not go
To share the love of God.
There's no mountain that's too high,
No land that seems too far.

For this love he will forsake
House and kin, and only take
Just what he needs
To feed the starving crowd.

For this love
What will you do,
Will you give your dearest treasures
For the gospel truth?

For this love,
Where will you go,
Have you been to the garden on your knees,
So the world will know.

For this love
the world became a place
Where desperate people need God's grace
For this love, he goes,
For this love, he knows he's doin' right,
So right.....

For this love
What will you do,
Will you give your dearest treasures
For the gospel truth?

For this love,
Where will you go,
Have you been to the garden on your knees,
So the world will know.

"The Scent of Roses"

by Ernestine Ladd, mother of former forwarding agent, Billy Ladd. Mrs. Ladd became "Mom" to Cecil, and she treated him like a son.

I have heard the old saying, "The fragrance always stays on the hands that give the roses."
If that is true then everyone knows --
That Cecil went into presence of God saturated in the scent of rose.
Cecil found joy in giving to others.
No one was a stranger to Cecil, they were all brothers.
Like the roses' sweet scent –
He carried the love of God wherever he went –
Sharing with others in word and in deed
Preaching the Word around the world
And helping the ones who were in need.
He shared his clothes, his food, his home –
And like God's own Son he gave his life before he went home
To stand with the martyrs around God's throne.
Somehow I think Heaven is sweeter since Cecil is there –
And the scent of roses is in the air.

Betty Bruce Tillery Byrd

Bruce. Who would ever name a baby girl Bruce? My parents, Wells Draughan Tillery II and Wilma Cozart Tillery, did. They were, however, highly influenced by my great-aunt, Sula Bett Williams. Great-Aunt Bett did not marry and had no children of her own. She and her sister, Ruby Tyree Williams, pretty much raised my dad and his sister, Gene, after his dad, Bruce Pennington Tillery, died when little Wells D. was seven years old. My dad's mother, Birdie Mae Williams Tillery, was distraught over her husband's early death from tuberculosis and thereafter led the life of a merry widow until she was married to Bob Anderson when I was just a toddler.

Great-Aunt Bett thought that it would be a fine idea to name me for herself--so she chose Betty as a derivation of her own name, Bett, and for the popular actress, Betty Grable. She also suggested that Bruce, after my grandfather, Bruce Pennington Tillery, would go nicely with Betty. Thus, on the day of my birth, April 29, 1948, in Roanoke Rapids, North Carolina, the baby girl born to Wells D. and Wilma became known as Betty Bruce Tillery. I have come across a number of Betty Byrds in my lifetime, but never have I met, nor heard of, another

Betty Bruce Tillery nor a Betty Bruce Byrd. Thanks, Daddy and Mama and Aunt Bett, for my unique name!

Maybe it was my name that set me apart early in life--made me just a little bit different, a bit of my own person. I loved school, and I loved to work. I liked bringing home stacks of books so that I could methodically make my way through homework at the big dining table that was set in front of the big picture window in our living room. I couldn't wait until I was old enough to mow the grass. I liked getting up early on summer mornings to pick butterbeans in our garden and then sit with my mother to shell them. One of the early highlights of my life was turning 12 years old and being deemed by my neighbors as old enough and responsible enough to babysit for pay. Then I was able to add my babysitting money to my grass-cutting money for my savings for college.

It seems like I spent much of high school dreaming about going to college and being a missionary. As I waited for that day to come, I was consumed by school and by church.

It was nice growing up in a small town. The town had a lot of history, as far as my family was concerned. My dad had always lived there, as had his grandfather, Wells Draughan Tillery. I loved driving by the big, two-story white house on Roanoke Avenue that had once belonged to my great-grandfather -- the house where Black Betty, the cook, made special food for my daddy when he was a little boy. My daddy had a lot of interaction with his grandfather, and he told me stories about him. He was the first mayor of Roanoke Rapids and one of the founders of the First Baptist Church in Roanoke Rapids. He had owned a really big farm, like a plantation, several miles out from Roanoke Rapids. I always thought that was really cool, because the little town where the plantation was has my maiden name, Tillery.

There were lots of African Americans in the county in which I lived. Some of them had my last name because they were descendants of the slaves who had worked on the Tillery plantation. In our bookcase at home, we had a hard-back book entitled The History of Halifax County. I loved reading that book because it was tied to my family.

When I was growing up, the schools in Roanoke Rapids were still segregated. The town was segregated, too. There was a section of Roanoke Rapids called Hodgestown. That is where African Americans lived. When I was in high school, Don Boyer, the minister at First Christian Church during those years, took a few of us in the youth group to Hodgestown to conduct a vacation Bible school. That was my first "mission trip." It really was a different world, and it was just across the street from my backyard. I loved the Negro spirituals they sang. The little children liked to touch my smooth, blonde hair and white hands. It was a foretaste of the years to come in Zambia.

It was fun growing up in the same town as my dad. I liked re-tracing the footsteps of where he grew up, played football, graduated from high school. I graduated from the same high school as he, even had a couple of the same

40

teachers -- like Miss Price in seventh grade. My dad was baptized at First Baptist Church with a group of his teenaged friends; I was baptized at First Christian Church all by myself. He said when he was baptized, it was "the thing to do" for the moment; for me, it was a life-long commitment to follow Christ.

After graduation from high school, my dad went off to the South Pacific to fight in World War II. When he came back from the war, he met my mother who had moved from her home town in Greenville, North Carolina, to teach school in Roanoke Rapids.

My mother had grown up in a family of nine children, and she was the second to last child. She had gone to college, at what is now East Carolina University, in the town in which she grew up. At the time she attended, it was strictly a college to train teachers and was known as East Carolina Teachers College. She had wanted to be a nurse, but her dad said that was not a proper profession for a woman.

My maternal grandmother, Hattie Mae Evans Cozart, was a religious person. She had been raised in the Primitive Baptist Church. She had really long hair and practiced foot-washing in the church. There was no Sunday school for her nine children, however, so Hattie Mae parceled them out to whatever Sunday school they could get to. As a child, my mother attended a Disciples of Christ Christian church, so when she came to Roanoke Rapids, she began going to First Christian Church in Roanoke Rapids.

My mom and dad were married on September 21, 1946. My dad traveled for his work as a right of way engineer for Virginia Electric and Power Company, and sometimes he was away from home for a whole week or more. Weekends were the only time he was home, and he didn't often feel like going to church on those days. My mother always cooked a big, Sunday dinner and, I think, all of that interfered with my parents going to church.

When my daddy would come home on the weekends, he would think it would be really great if we would do something as a family. We used to go on picnics in the summer, but we'd have to go to places that were miles away, like Buggs Island Dam in Virginia. My dad would get home on Friday night, recover from the work week on Saturday, and then we'd go on the picnic on Sunday.

As I got a little older, I thought, "Ooh, this isn't right. We're going on picnics and not going to church." So I started asking if we could go to church first, but that really made it impossible to go any distance away for a picnic. I was unhappy to go on picnics if it meant missing church. That put a dent in our happy family picnics. So, from then on, I was somewhat like a fanatic child in the eyes of my parents. I think my mother was afraid I would grow up to be like our neighbor who never cut her hair, wore only dresses with long sleeves, and was always trying to convert my mother who must have appeared to need converting because she wore shorts and sleeveless blouses around the house. So, when I was 16, and still not into wearing make-up, my mother sat me down on the bed and said, "You ARE going to wear lipstick."

I think I caused my parents a lot of worry and frustration. Between not wearing lipstick, wanting to go to church instead of picnics, and not going to school dances, perhaps I had turned out to be a pretty disappointing daughter. I was a very serious person. All I wanted to do was school work, church, and teach in youth group and Sunday school class.

Finally, I graduated from high school and was ready to go to Bible college. I studied hard, worked in the kitchen and in the library, sang in a trio, and traveled on weekends to represent the school. I was very happy working toward achieving the purpose to which I believed God had called me, to give my life in service as a missionary to Africa.

We

Courtship

At the beginning of my junior year in college, I was pitched a ball that I didn't see coming. Cecil Byrd arrived on the Johnson Bible College campus in August, 1968. He worked on campus for a couple of weeks before school started. My dearly beloved roommate, Mary Frances Followell, had arrived early to work before the beginning of the school year as well and had the pleasure of meeting Cecil before I did.

When my parents pulled up on the Johnson Bible College campus to deliver me for my junior year, they parked beside the telephone booth next to Bell Hall. That was a fateful moment. Cecil was in that phone booth. One glance in his direction and I knew that my resolution to swear off men during my junior year in college had just gone out the window. I looked at him and thought, "Oh, my goodness! He is my destiny."

It didn't help that Mary's first words to me were, "BettaLou, you've got to meet this new guy on campus. I think you're going to marry him. He is perfect for you." Her conjecture probably had to do with the ultra-serious personalities she was trying to match-make.

Mary did introduce me to Cecil. About a week later, when I was walking back to the dorm from the laundry room, Cecil walked up beside me and took the heavy laundry basket I was carrying. He took it back to the dorm for me, and then we walked around the big block on campus. That was a sure sign on the campus of Johnson Bible College that a couple was officially "going together." Our "going together" all happened on campus as Cecil had no money and no car. We walked around the block frequently, ate together in the dining room, and talked at night before curfew on the benches in front of Bell Hall. We broke up around Thanksgiving, only to be reunited that summer when we exchanged several letters during my internship in Canada.

42

When we returned to campus in the fall, it was as if we had never broken up the year before.

When I began the first semester of my senior year at Johnson, Cecil was a first-semester sophomore. He was busy with studies, week-end ministry, basketball, and work-study. I was studying hard, working in the school library and several hours in the afternoon and evening at the Boys Club in South Knoxville. My college years, so I thought, would soon come to an end. By taking heavy class loads and a few additional classes in the summer by correspondence, I would need only eight more credit hours to graduate at the end of the spring semester.

I was exhausted. Maybe it was because, due to an internship in Canada the previous summer, I hadn't had a summer to somewhat recuperate from the previous year. Maybe it was the extra job at the Boys' Club. This was the first semester that I had worked off-campus. Between classes, the library job on campus, and the Boys' Club job off-campus, I wasn't able to start homework or studying until after 10 each night.

Toward the end of the semester, I said to Cecil, "You know what? I am so tired. I'm going back to North Carolina and finishing my last semester by correspondence. Then I won't have to work two jobs and study half the night for eight hours worth of credits."

He replied, "Don't go home. Let's get married instead."

Planning for Marriage

I can't remember what day that "proposal" occurred; but just a few weeks afterward, we got married. It took a little working out and re-arranging to make it happen. Cecil had already planned to return to California during Christmas break. He had a year and a half of Bible college under his belt, and he was ready to evangelize his friends in Los Angeles. Robert, the man with whom Cecil had lived in California, was planning to purchase Cecil's plane ticket to L.A. and back to Knoxville. When Cecil told him that he was getting married and wanted to bring his wife, Robert said he would pay one way for each of us. Cecil arranged for us to hitch a ride to California with fellow students, Tom and Jettie Wymore, who were driving from Knoxville to San Bernadino, and Robert purchased tickets for us to fly back to Knoxville. With the honeymoon arrangements in place, we then planned the wedding and made a quick trip to North Carolina and Virginia to meet the parents.

The next two weeks were filled with requesting permission from the Dean of Students to marry in the middle of a school year, receiving marriage counseling from the same Dean of Students, being blessed by two wedding showers, and studying for semester exams.

The day before our wedding, I was in the library studying for my last exam when I was approached by four of my best male friends. They asked me NOT to get married. Did they know something I didn't know? If they did, they wouldn't say, and I was so gullibly in love that it wouldn't have mattered anyhow.

Wedding

When we discussed what kind of wedding to have, I won. Cecil and I were married in a private ceremony (I NEVER wanted to have to walk down an aisle in a church full of people where I was the center of attention with everyone looking at me). We were joined in holy matrimony on the last day of the semester, December 19, 1969, at 1:00 p.m in the basement of the Johnson Bible College home of Dr. and Mrs. Robert E. Black. Dr. Black was Dean of Students and Professor of Old Testament.

Cecil had finished his exams the day before, but I still had one to go (Systematic Theology) at 10:00 a.m. on my wedding day. I successfully completed the exam (got an A!) in time to run back to my dorm room to don my cute little winter white A-line wool dress with a Peter Pan collar and three tiny black buttons down the middle below the collar. When I look at the pictures, the dress seems a little short; it couldn't have been that short, though, or I never would have worn it on the Johnson Bible College campus, especially in the presence of the Dean of Students, who was very strict about such matters. Mary, my roommate, did my hair. I was ready when Cecil picked me up at the dorm to escort me (walking, of course, as neither of us owned a car) to Dr. Black's house. Mary, as my maid of honor, accompanied us to the house where we were greeted by Dr. and Mrs. Black and the Sabens family. Mike Sabens was Cecil's best man, and Mike's wife, Jane, and their girls accompa-

nied him. Dr. Black performed the ceremony, which ended with the Mizpah Benediction, in front of the fireplace of Dr. Black's new home. We exchanged rings, kissed each other for the second time in our whole lives, and were ready to make our way to California.

Honeymoon

After the ceremony, we went back to the dorms to pick up our luggage. Tom and Jettie, along with Joe Finnell, who was catching a ride to El Centro, picked us up, and we were on our way. Four hours later, we found ourselves in Nashville with the car broken down. It was after five on a Friday afternoon, and all the parts places were closed. Nothing was open.

Tom and Jettie called their parents who bought tickets to fly them the rest of the way to California the next morning. That left Cecil, Joe, and me to figure out how to get to California or to return to Knoxville. In the meantime, the man who towed the car took us all to a nearby, dumpy motel. There were holes in the sheets and, in Joe's room, a mouse who nibbled on Joe's open bag of potato chips. This was not the perfect setting for one's wedding night; but it was a wedding night, nonetheless.

During the night, Joe called Coach Morgan at Johnson Bible College. Coach and Mrs. Morgan agreed to drive Joe's pick-up truck to Nashville the next morning. When the Morgans arrived with Joe's pick-up truck, the three of us jumped in and never stopped again--except for fuel--until we reached El Centro.

Mr. and Mrs. Finnell had made arrangements for Cecil and me to stay in the apartment of the church's youth director for a couple of days while she was away. They had also planned a small wedding reception which Joe's family and a few members of the church attended.

While we were in El Centro, Tom and Jettie came by in Tom's jeep and took us pheasant hunting in the desert. I just rode in the jeep. I didn't fire a gun. The next day we headed to Los Angeles to spend Christmas and the rest of our honeymoon with Cecil's friend, Robert.

Our first argument occurred in Los Angeles. The groundwork was laid in Robert's kitchen. Robert had gone to work, and I was cooking my first breakfast for Cecil. I wonder why I thought I could cook in the first place. Did I think that the gift of cooking was miraculously bestowed on the bride when the officiant said, "I now pronounce you man and wife"?

Cecil's words were, "Betty, these eggs aren't done. The white's too runny."

Those words cut me to the heart! I had failed my husband, so I cried.

He, who had been cooking for his brothers and sister for years, instructed me in the proper way to cook eggs, and no divorce papers were filed. After all, eggs aren't grounds for divorce.

Other than learning to cook, the highlights of our honeymoon in Los Angeles included celebrating Christmas with Robert (he addressed his gift to me as "Prima"), going to church in L.A., watching Cecil play basketball at the church, having dinner with Cecil's former employer in Santa Monica, and spending a day at Disneyland. When those events concluded, we made our way back to Knoxville (via Chicago) and began our lives as a married couple on the campus of Johnson Bible College.

Newlyweds

We got back from Los Angeles on a very, very cold night in January. It seemed strange to be coming back to where we would be living together. Our room was a corner room in Bell Hall--right next to the telephone booth where I first saw Cecil. We could actually look out one window and see that telephone booth.

There was a bench under the window where couples usually sat, and we had sat on that bench, of course, in the past – but not closer than 18 inches because that was the rule at Johnson in the '60s. In our room, we had a bed, a desk, and a dresser that belonged to the school. Cecil's desk was right at the window at the front of the building. The bed was at the side of the desk, and the dresser was against the wall behind the desk. We could sit on the edge of the bed and touch the desk and the dresser at the same time. That's how close everything was. In front of Cecil's desk was the little, bitty sink and fridge combination with a

little tiny stove next to it. The school librarian, who lived across the hall from us, gave us a small table at which we could eat. She had antiqued it green and didn't need it for her apartment anymore. We had a closet with sliding doors, and that's all. I don't think we even had a bookshelf. The bathrooms were down the hall – one for men and one for women.

Mike Sabens had picked us up from the airport. We had flown from Los Angeles to Chicago and then on to Knoxville. They took us down to their cottage on the river for chili before driving us up to our little "apartment" in Bell Hall.

On Monday, I started looking for a job, and Cecil went back to school for his second semester sophomore year. Since I only needed eight more credit hours to graduate, I planned to work until the last semester of Cecil's senior year and then take the classes I needed to graduate with him.

It wasn't that easy to find a job. I started out working at a dry cleaners on Chapman Highway. The owner had hired other Johnson Bible College students before and was open to having Johnson Bible College students, but he said to me, "You won't last here because you almost have your degree from college, and why would anyone with a degree from college want to work in a dry cleaners?" I was desperate for a job, so I said, "Oh, yes, I do want to work here!" He was right, however. I did not like working there; but I would have kept on except I lost someone's pants. Or, at least they thought I lost someone's pants. None of us could find them anywhere. I was really sad about that. I started looking for another job, because I hated being the person who lost people's pants

They didn't fire me, so I had to keep working there until I found another job--even though I hated it more as each day passed.

I went to the Tennessee State Employment Agency, which really was a good deal, because you didn't have to pay them. They gave me a skills test and then sent me out on job interviews. I went on two interviews. The first interview was at the University of Tennessee. They gave me a typing test and said that I scored higher for speed and accuracy than anyone they had ever before interviewed. When I went for the department interview, they said, "We just need to let you know that we'll need you to pretend to be busy, because we don't always have something for you to do. During exam time, or crunch times of the year, we'll need you. But we don't really need you the whole school year, so we'll need you to be able to act like you're busy." I wasn't very happy about that, although it did sound like an easy job. It would have been so easy to work there because another girl at school worked at the University of Tennessee, and I would have a ride to and from work with her.

My second interview was the next day with an insurance company. I must have scored well on their test, too, because they also wanted to hire me. Between the two jobs, I chose the insurance company because there I wouldn't have to act like I was busy. Little did I know, however, that I would be expected to laugh at jokes I didn't think were funny!

Working at the insurance company meant that the girl who worked at U.T. had to drop me on the street corner where she turned toward the campus, and I had to walk forever to get to Prudential every morning, and then I had to walk back in the afternoon for her to pick me up. I became the new business clerk. I worked with Evelyn, who was the office manager, and Dianne, who was the secretary to the director. A second reason I chose Prudential was because the office manager told me she was a Christian. She was married to a deacon in a Baptist church. The branch manager was also a deacon in a Baptist church. The office manager was pleased that I was a Christian.

It was a rude awakening to me not many weeks later when I realized that I had taken the job that was more difficult to get to and which paid less so that I could work in an office with all Christians, only to find out that all people don't have the same ideas as to what it means to live as a Christian.

Most of the salesmen in the office smoked, and they didn't have any qualms about blowing smoke all over me when I took their new applications for insurance at the counter. When I'd get home in the afternoon, Cecil would say, "You smell like cigarettes." There were no bans on smoking in public in those days!

Besides smoking, they also told off-color jokes and flirted with the women in the office. This was an eye-opening experience for me.

One of my responsibilities as the new business clerk was to take care of the accounting for the campaigns that went on between agencies in the district. The branch manager asked me at one point early in my career to enter into the campaign records policies that had been written before the campaign began. I said I couldn't do that because that wasn't honest. He called me in his office and said, "Now that you're in the business world, you need to know that everything is not black and white. Some things are gray. And you need to be able to work in those gray areas." I said, "No, I can't do that. It's not right." For some reason, once again, I didn't get fired; but, from then on, the office manager kept the campaign records.

I worked at the insurance company for a year and a half, until I was a couple of months away from giving birth to my first child. They had hoped that I would not have a baby that soon, but they still gave me a beautiful yellow baby quilt and pillow and came to visit me in the hospital when Ben was born and asked me to bring him to the office when we were out of the hospital. I did. They thought he was beautiful – which he was!

Adjusting to marriage and work at the same time wasn't as easy as I thought it would be. I was trying to learn to cook, too, and it was hard because I had to catch a ride to work at 6:30 in the morning. Being a very dutiful wife, I always wanted to get up and fix breakfast. Cecil, not being a morning person, did not want to get up and eat it. That caused a little bit of tension until I came to the realization, "Well, what's the need for me to cook if he doesn't want to eat at that time?" That solved that problem.

I didn't get home in the afternoons until after 6:00, which was a bit of a trial because Cecil had to be a chapel at 7. My trying to read a cook book and figure out how to cook something to eat in a hurry was a problem.

I had to hurry up and try and cook in my own slow way. I had a Betty Crocker "Dinner for Two" cookbook that my grandmother had given me. That helped a lot. I was really embarrassed when Cecil asked one of my professors to come and teach me how to make strawberry pie, though. For some reason, that embarrassed me (enough to make me cry). It seemed like I wasn't doing well as a wife. I was lacking in essential skills. It didn't sit well that I cried, either.

We did, however, survive those newlywed years, and life became sweeter and sweeter.

Into All
the World

September 12, 1976

Until this day in history, neither Cecil nor I had ever left the North American continent. I had crossed the border of the United States into Alberta, Canada, for a 1969 summer's internship in Grande Prairie. Cecil had cross-countried from Virginia to California. That was the extent of our travels. Then the day came: September 12, 1976.

We had been spending our last days in the U. S. at my parents' home in North Carolina. My mom and dad were planning to drive us to Richmond, Virginia, 80 miles to the north, to catch our flight, leaving in the evening of that bright, sunny Sunday. We went to church, came home, and partook of Sunday dinner. My mother always cooked a very nice Sunday dinner of beef roast, fried chicken, or baked chicken in gravy.

I remember being dressed up in a white dress (what was I thinking?) with a little red polka dot scarf. Cecil was dressed in a suit as was Ben, who was four years old. Miriam was wearing her little green plaid dress with a white collar. My dad had gone to his bedroom after lunch to take a nap. When it was time to go, we went to get him, saying excitedly, "Let's go!"

He was lying on the bed and wouldn't get up. He said he wasn't going to take us to the airport. Since he was not prone to expressing his emotions (except anger, perhaps), it was really quite shocking that he wouldn't get up to take us to the airport – that he was that upset or sad.

My sister, rescuing us as she has on many occasions, said that she would drive us to the airport, so we did manage to get to Richmond. My mother had cried for years already, thinking about the day that I would go away to Africa. Now it was actually happening. Tearful good-byes were exchanged between my sister and mother and our family, and we got on the airplane that took us to New York where we boarded a Trans World Airways plane to Paris. In Paris, we spent the next twelve hours trying to sleep in a day room before boarding a UTA flight to Lusaka, Zambia. It was no longer September 12, and we were far from the only country and people we had ever really known.

Prostrate in Paris

The long hours in the day room passed, and we finally found ourselves in the lobby of the hotel. Cecil was checking out at the desk while I stood across the lobby holding not yet two-year-old Miriam on my hip, anxiously watching for the bus that would take us to the airport where we would board a plane for the next leg of the journey. Through the big glass doors, I saw a bus approaching and slowing to a stop. Fearing we would miss the bus, I began running across the lobby to hurry Cecil up at the desk. The next thing I knew, I had tripped on a rug and was lying sprawled on the lobby floor with Miriam beneath me. The bus was pulling away from the curb.

That's okay. It wasn't our bus.

From Paris to Lusaka

Our bus finally did come, and we got on it with no further incident. It took us to our plane – the UTA plane – that was going to take us to Lusaka. This part of the trip I remember because of the food that was served – very hard rolls. It must have been a French thing, because I had never eaten such hard rolls before. After you cracked the rolls open, the bread inside was soft, but the outside certainly wasn't.

Miriam was into kicking her feet and ended up kicking the chair in front of us. That wasn't very pleasant for the people in front of us, so the man in the chair requested that she stop.

Eventually, we landed in Douala, Cameroon, for re-fueling. Our itinerary had not mentioned that we would be landing anywhere between Paris and Lusaka. People came in and sprayed for whatever it is they sprayed for on planes in those days. Just before we landed, a stewardess came through and said, "Are you going to Douala?" Well, I thought she was saying "Ndola," which was our final destination, so I said, "Yes." But at least she didn't make us get off when we got to Douala because it wouldn't have been good to be on the ground in Douala with no place to go!

Some people did get off the plane in Douala, however, and that left several empty seats for the rest of us. There was room to stretch out and lie down. That was a big mistake, however, because I think lying across the seat with Miriam made me airsick. I learned the hard way that it made her airsick, too.

Welcome to Lusaka: Blap!

Eventually, as the sun rose, we descended on the red, red soil of Zambia. The Davises and Delaneys, Zambia Christian Mission missionaries living in Lusaka, were waiting to meet and greet us. They helped us through our first experience with customs and immigration, and soon we were experiencing our first scary drive on the "wrong" side of the road as we traveled to the home of Don and Linda Mechem, also ZCM missionaries living in Lusaka. Linda had prepared a lovely meal. As we all stood around on the kitchen floor greeting one another, Miriam's queasy stomach got the best of her, and she threw up right in the middle of the circle. Welcome to Lusaka!

We spent the next two days on the farm inhabited by the Davises and Delaneys outside of Lusaka. Ben, at four years old, immediately fell in love with Robin Delaney, despite the fact that she was several years his senior.

During the two days in Lusaka, Don Mechem sold us a truck, and we drove to Ndola -- our home for the next fifteen years.

The Blue-headed Lizard

When we arrived in Ndola, we went to the apartment of Kay Watts Moll. Kay and I met in college. Her first husband, Eddie Watts, was killed in a car accident during the first year of their marriage. After Eddie's death, Kay went to Zambia to work with the Davises. They built on an apartment at the end of their house at 16 Kuomoboka Crescent for Kay to live in while she taught Bible in the schools in Zambia. Kay had prepared lunch for us and had invited the Connellys and the Brants, who were also a part of Zambia Christian Mission and lived about 50 kilometers away in the town of Kitwe.

Later in the afternoon, Ben and Miriam and the two Connelly girls, Christy and April, were playing outside while the adults chatted in Kay's living room. Ben came running in, shouting, "Mama! Mama! Come and see what's out here."

I ran outside, and there saw for the first time in my life, up close and personal, a blue-headed lizard, perched on a tree stump, darting his tongue in and out. I screamed and screamed. The first shock of being in Africa (after riding on the "wrong" side of the road) was seeing that creature.

The next day, Charlie Delaney, who had escorted us from Lusaka to Ndola, took Cecil to the bank to open an account. He also introduced us to the local evangelist, Ba Mutyoka. Charlie returned to Lusaka, and we were ready to do mission work in Ndola.,

We stayed with Kay for a couple of weeks while we painted and cleaned our house at 12 Katutwa Road. Afterward, we were able to unpack our crates and move into our tan cinder block house with cement floors. I loved the bush-grass fence and the elephant statues at the gate, but I still did not like those blue-headed lizards that crawled around everywhere.

Keeping the Home Fires Burning

We began to settle into our house and into life in Zambia. I thought that I would be involved in Bible studies and literacy work among women from dawn to dusk. Cecil had other ideas. He said, "Betty, I need you to stay with the children and keep the home fires burning."

Being a fairly submissive wife at the time, I did that. I did become involved in attending and sometimes leading a weekly English-speaking Bible study in my neighborhood part of town and enjoyed Sundays in the local churches. It certainly did take a great amount of time to shop in the markets and so many different shops (there not being one grocery that would have even all of the basic pantry items) and then cook it all from scratch, scratch, scratch. I had to learn to make bread, tomato sauce, white sauce, discover how to cook cabbage a thousand different ways, shop daily due to not having a fridge for a while, etc. etc. etc. So, my time at home was fruitful. Time passed quickly.

As we began settling into life in Zambia and completed a period of language study, Cecil said to me, "Do you want to go with me to the villages on certain days?"

My dream was coming true!

Early Ministry in Zambia

Ba Mutyoka, the local evangelist, introduced Cecil to the eight existing Ndola churches, four in townships and four in rural areas within a fifty-mile radius of the city. He was also very helpful in teaching us the locations and meeting times of these churches.

After finishing a period of language study and becoming acquainted with the churches, Cecil began classes – leadership training by extension – going from one church to one church to one church, training and teaching leaders who would carry on the work.

When Gary and Meta Burlington joined the Ndola work in 1977, Gary

began working with the four township churches and Cecil with the four rural churches. That made it easy to devote one training day per week to each of the rural churches--all of whom were blessed with leaders who were able to take a day off from work in the fields each week to attend leadership training classes.

We continued to rotate among the churches on Sundays. The whole family would go. We would usually leave the house between 7:00 and 8:00 on Sunday morning, spend the whole day in the village, and come home starving. On those Sundays, Cecil would help me cook. I would fry chicken, and he would peel potatoes and make gravy. The children would pick lemons from our lemon tree, and we would make lemonade. After Dwayne Hicks spent a summer with us as an intern in 1981 (among other things, teaching me to make biscuits like his mother did), I would make the best biscuits ever (before that, I made biscuits, too -- but not the best biscuits ever). By the time we ate dinner and cleaned up the dishes, it was time for bed.

Hard Times

You might call these early days in Zambia "hard times" because the borders between Zambia and Zimbabwe were closed due to the war in Zimbabwe. There were no imports coming into the country, so it was like subsistence living. There was very little bread. There was rarely bread in the bakery. There were very few commodities in the stores. In fact, it was hard to get anything you needed. So, in the hours when Cecil was free from classes, he began to build relationships (he was very good at that!) with business men and Indian shopkeepers. Because of these relationships, sometimes we were able to buy 50kg bags of flour from a shopkeeper or make a four hour drive to Lusaka to buy flour from the mill (after standing for hours in long lines).

There were no dairy products, either. It was a very exciting day if someone would call (when the phones were working) or drop by and say, "There's milk (or butter) at the Dairy Board!"

Then we would rush to the Dairy Board, and there would be so many people mobbed outside. Sometimes we'd get some; other times we wouldn't.

Same thing with cooking oil or sugar--all of the basic commodities (even maize meal, the staple of Zambia)--you didn't get it unless you knew somebody personally or you stood in mobs or long lines for hours at a time. Beef and pork, too--Buy a cow or pig and butcher it yourself or you didn't have it. Raise your own chickens for eggs and for meat. Make your own bread, if you could buy the flour and cooking oil and yeast to make it (at least yeast could be mailed to us in care packages)!

But we did have Zambian-made peanut butter. Crunchy would not be the word for it. I think the word would be THICK. The oil floated for about half an inch on top. Sometimes you could mix it back in, but it still turned out THICK and non-spreadable. You could tear up a piece of your precious, homemade bread in no time flat trying to spread that peanut butter. Cecil usually packed a lunch of very, very hard Zambian ginger snaps, a jar of very, very THICK Zambian peanut butter, bananas from our banana tree (when there were bananas on it), and two bottles of warm Coke for lunch in the villages each day. During mango season, he had it made, however. With an abundance of mango trees in every village, hunger was staved off for awhile for everyone. Eventually, I got a blender with a grinder which made it possible to make our own peanut butter during groundnut season, but the yield did not really make the effort worthwhile.

We could usually get cabbage and tomatoes and onions. I learned to make many cabbage recipes, and, of course, how to make tomato sauce, tomato salsa, tomato everything as well as mayonnaise, soybean sandwich spread, pizza dough (pretty much like bread dough!), avocado ice cream, anything and everything from scratch--as long as you could get the basic ingredients to start with. My best investment ever was the *More with Less*

Cookbook, published by the Mennonite brethren. We definitely had less, and we needed more!

In addition to the banana trees and mango trees and one lemon tree already growing in our yard, we planted tangerine, orange, and guava trees. They all bore fruit quickly. Of course, we planted a garden. What a blessing were all those free seeds to missionaries from Burpee Seed Company! That helped with food, and the flowers grown from the donated seeds were beautiful.

Once, when somebody gave us coffee beans, I planted them, too, and the plants from them bore enough to make a few pots of coffee. By this time, we had missionary friends in the Eastern Province where Zambian coffee was grown, and we were able to get our coffee supply through them. Even when goods were available, distribution was a problem. We would sometimes "trade" what was available in our area for what was available in another area.

Oh, yes, and I also grew sunflowers, but I only tried to harvest the seeds once. Once is enough for some experiences--and we really could exist without snacking on sunflower seeds.

Churches and the Work

Along with the vegetables, fruit trees, and flowers, the churches also grew and grew and grew. The churches in that area had an annual conference in which all came together for a few days of preaching and teaching. The women also had a yearly conference for a shorter period of time. It was exciting to be a part of those gatherings and to be invited to preach and teach and to share in the cooking and partaking of local foods. I was, however, so happy when one little old lady did not want to share her fuzzy caterpillars with anyone (especially me!).

After being on the field for three months, Cecil wrote the plans for the first full year of ministry in 1977 to include: (1) training clinics for elders and deacons (2) teachings on stewardship, tithing, and offerings (3) lessons on how to teach (4) daily Bible studies with the churches (5) more preaching conferences (6) prayer for more conversions and laborers for the harvest (7) learn to write and speak in Lamba.

More and more churches were started through initiatives of the existing churches and church leaders. By the time we left Zambia in 1991, forty churches had been established within that 50-mile radius in which we worked in the villages around Ndola. The same was happening in Lusaka, Kitwe, Luanshya, Mufulira, the Eastern Province, the Western Province, and the Northern Province. God mightily blessed the work in Zambia. Praise His Name!

Zaire

Zambia borders the country of Zaire. In the Copperbelt Province, in which we lived in the city of Ndola, Zambia, there was a church that we visited frequently – Chibwabwa, which means "cabbage leaves." Of course, as you can guess from the name, a lot of cabbage was grown in that area. Cabbage was an oft-eaten vegetable in Zambia.

Chibwabwa was one of the first churches in which I was privileged to teach women to read. I went to the Ministry of Education, and they had literacy books made in Zambia. They were not the best planned books from a linguistics viewpoint. They were planned more like Dick and Jane readers. Just words. Sight words, we would call them. Even at that, however, I was so happy when I was able to purchase those books from the Ministry of Education. I started teaching the women at Chibwabwa how to read in the Bemba language because the Bemba primers were available, and most people understood and spoke Bemba, one of the five major languages in Zambia. We had studied Lamba, but there were no Lamba readers produced by the Ministry of Education; however, Lamba and Bemba were very similar languages with the same structure and approximately 40% the same in vocabulary. There was a mixture of Bemba and Lamba spoken on the Copperbelt.

I was able to go with Cecil to Chibwabwa to teach literacy and Bible and sewing to the women while he taught Bible and leadership training courses to the men. In the sewing classes, the women learned how to make quilts--not quilts that you would "quilt," but quilts that you piece together by hand and then sew a back on and tie each square with yarn. Finding blankets to purchase was a big problem in Zambia, and it could get quite cold in Zambia during the winter months of May, June, and July. The ladies loved making quilts. The classes were going very well until one of the ladies stole my scissors. Cecil said, "Betty, you cannot go back again until whoever stole the scissors brings them back." What an ordeal! Eventually, though, the lady who stole the scissors returned them and repented, so I was able to resume classes there.

Just behind the Chibwabwa church was the border to Zaire. We could very illegally cross into Zaire through the bush, if we had wanted to do so. It was fun, though, to be able to stand with one foot in Zambia and one foot in Zaire.

Cecil legally crossed into Zaire on several occasions to meet with some of the brothers who had put out a Macedonian call. Some of the Zairean church leaders came into Zambia and asked Cecil if he would come into Zaire and teach them. They had heard of the work that was going on in Zambia. Cecil went on several occasions to conduct seminars in Zaire. It was hard, though, because at the legal points of immigration, there was so much corruption. It became very costly to go because the border officials demanded huge bribes. When this happened, Cecil was no longer able to cross over into Zaire.

Malawi

Malawi, a country to the east of Zambia, was a beautiful, beautiful place with a myriad of lakes and tea plantations. During our early years in Zambia, Malawi was often a place we headed to for vacations or team meetings and retreats. President Banda reigned as President for Life in Malawi. The country enforced a strict dress code. Women were not allowed to wear pants, and their dresses had to be longer – at least reaching below the knees. Sleeveless tops and dresses were also banned.

I remember two vacations in Malawi. One was not long after Kathy was born. Some of our co-workers were saying, "You need to get away." I'm not sure what they saw in me that I wasn't recognizing. Perhaps I was experiencing a bit of post-partum depression, having given birth under stressful conditions far away from family and friends (except for our fellow missionaries, of course!).

Kay Watts fixed us a beautiful picnic lunch (including deviled eggs!) and we started out on the 12-hour journey to Monkey Bay in Malawi. Our first stop, however, was to visit the Davises and Delaneys on their farm outside of Lusaka. They had prepared a beautiful meal for us, too. I remember that the dessert was pavlova, created by Betty Delaney. I believe I cried that night because everyone was so kind.

The next day we continued on to Monkey Bay, finally arriving at our destination – a thatched-roof rondoval right on the shore of Lake Malawi. Ben and Miriam spent a lot of time playing at the water's edge and watching the little monkeys that lived in the trees all around the bay. Cecil fished, and I washed diapers by hand. At least, it was a beautiful, peaceful setting, seemingly far away from the worries of the world. On the way back to Ndola, we stopped in Blantyre to visit the Brants, who had since moved there from Kitwe, and the Ellericks, with whom we spent a couple of days. We all returned to Ndola rested and recovered and happy to be home (where I had a washing machine!). That Maytag washer and dryer set was one of the best purchases we ever made. It washed many a missionary's clothes, and we never needed a repairman for the entire fifteen years we used it!

About three years later, the mission planned a retreat in Malawi. Meta Burlington and I were both pregnant, expecting babies in January of 1982. While everyone else was in Malawi, Meta and I hung out in Ndola. The highlight of our time together was watching Princess Diana's wedding on Zambian TV.

A few years after that, we went on a family vacation to Grand Beach, which was also a part of Lake Malawi. Unlike Monkey Bay, however, there was an undertow in the water. Grand Beach actually looked like a beach on the ocean, with waves in which one could almost body surf. I loved listening to the waves crash on the shore as we lay in our bed with the windows open in our little cottage at night. I love that sound!

The undertow was quite strong, however. Ben became our hero when he pulled Kathy out from its grip. Kathy owes her life to Ben!

Ill in Israel

Our first three-year term in Zambia came and went. It was time for furlough. We booked our tickets to the U.S. via Israel. Those were the glorious days of traveling when you could book so many stops in a trip without extra charges. Here was our chance to see the Holy Land.

Our first walking tour in Jerusalem was inside the walls. The markets were beautiful. There was so much luscious fruit. It seems we had been deprived of fruit for nearly three years--at least the kinds we saw in the markets in Israel. It was easy to imagine the spies carrying grapes back to prove that the Promised Land really was a land flowing with milk and honey. Yes, I knew I shouldn't eat the fruit from the market--but it was so tempting. I succumbed to those luscious grapes and crisp apples. Then I paid for it by being confined to my room, very sick to my stomach for a whole twenty-four hours. I learned my lesson and missed the walking tour outside the walls of Jerusalem.

Miriam also found Israel a little tough on her stomach. We ended up washing her little dress in the Sea of Galilee after she threw up on it and the touring car we had booked. I have never forgotten that incident nor the looks of our companions in the car.

Frantic in Frankfort

After the brief stop in Israel, we spent our first furlough year in Campbellsville, Kentucky. It was good to see everyone again. I remember how cold I was that winter. My blood must have thinned after three years in the tropics! Besides that, our bedroom was an afterthought to the little house that we rented. I doubt that the city ever inspected that addition to the house. It was very, very drafty.

The year passed quickly, with Cecil traveling much of the time alone as Ben was then in third grade and Miriam in kindergarten. Six straight weeks of chicken pox took care of most of the spring. Miriam brought it home first. When she cleared up two weeks later, Ben broke out. Two weeks after that, Kathy was all speckled with pox. We even missed Easter Sunday at church, but they all dressed up in their Easter best and posed with their Easter baskets for their Easter pictures. That window of opportunity only came every three years.

The year in the U. S. ended, and we returned to Zambia via Frankfurt, Germany, loaded down with ten suitcases, at least half of which contained Muppets made by ladies at Bloomington Christian Church in Byrdstown, Tennessee, to be used in youth work in Zambia. We were scheduled to spend the night in Frankfurt in order to make our connecting flight, and it was necessary to claim our checked baggage.

Baggage claim was in an area below ground level. After claiming baggage, it was necessary to ascend a level to get out of the airport. For some reason, we could not find the elevators, so Cecil decided to attempt an ascent by escalator. This was no easy feat with three children and all of those suitcases.

Realizing that he might encounter some difficulty, Cecil instructed me to wait at the bottom of the escalator with the children while he attempted to escalate with a luggage cart piled high with suitcases. I obeyed, watching anxiously from the bottom of the escalator. All went well until Cecil reached the top.

Suddenly, I was watching Cecil jogging in place at the top of the escalator. What a funny sight it was from the bottom – the luggage carrier stuck at the top and Cecil's feet running in place. I started laughing and couldn't stop. Cecil, on the other hand, was far from laughing.

After several seconds of jogging, he literally threw the luggage cart. Suitcases went flying everywhere. It is a wonder, indeed, that Cecil was not charged with attempted murder.

To further complicate matters, Cecil was carrying our onward tickets and passports in his back pocket. Somehow they got caught in the side of the escalator. A man (who was not overcome with laughter) standing beside me at the bottom of the escalator had the foresight to push the button which stops the escalator. Perhaps if it all hadn't been so hilarious, I would have thought of that myself.

We then retrieved the tickets, passports, and scattered suitcases and went on our merry way. I continued to laugh the night away in our bed in Frankfurt, waking myself several times during the night in delirious giggling fits.

Robbed in Botswana

The month was June, 1984, returning from our second furlough. We had flown into Johannesburg to pick up two trucks – one new white Isuzu and one used blue something (sorry, I'm not very good at remembering the makes of foreign vehicles!). Because of his previous criminal record, Cecil was a prohibited immigrant to Zimbabwe. That meant we had to drive through Botswana in order to get from South Africa to Zambia. Botswana is mostly desert, the Kalahari Desert. There wasn't much to see on the drive except for sand and ostriches. I have a very clear picture of why ostriches burying their heads in the sand is a good metaphor.

After traveling miles and miles and miles on the paved road through the desert, seeing very few cars besides ours, we stopped at a cute little place with chalets on stilts outside of Francistown. After carrying in the luggage we needed for the night, we walked across to the restaurant. We ate ostrich for the first (and only) time in our lives!

After the delicious meal, we went back to the chalets and found that our belongings had been stolen! This consisted of all the stuff we were bringing back from furlough. I even had my first pair of prescription sunglasses – something I had dreamed about all of my adult life. All of our new things had been stolen; but worst of all, our passports were missing as well. That meant that we would have to turn around and go all that way back through the desert to Gaborone, because Gaborone was the capital and the only place we could get new passports.

The chalet owners said, "Well, before you turn around, let's search all the places around here." The next morning we started searching. Some of the searchers eventually found that the contents of Cecil's briefcase had been dumped in a dry river bed, so at least we had our passports back. We were able to get back in our cars and resume our journey. Praise God that we got those passports back!

We drove the rest of the way to Zambia. We parked the vehicles in the driveway, and my little blue pickup truck (I believe it may have been a Peugeot) never started again. But I will always be able to say that I drove a little blue pickup truck through the Kalahari Desert. Quite a feat!

Kenya

Kenya is an East African country through which we had to fly on several occasions to get to and from Zambia. When we did, we would stop over to visit our friends, Larry and Judy Niemeyer, whom we had first met in Zambia. They had lived about 12 hours north of us in the Northern Province of Zambia during our first term of service from 1976-1979. When they would come to Ndola for shopping, they stayed with us. They left Zambia at the end of our first term there and moved to Kenya where they started another ministry.

Kenya is also where Ben went to boarding school at Rift Valley Academy in eighth and ninth grades and where we attended the Pan Africa Missionary Conference at Brackenhurst. I remember that conference in Brackenhurst very well because that was when I was first pregnant with Deborah. I was so sick. Nobody knew I was pregnant, except for Cecil. We had to ride in the back of a Jeep Pajero around and around those hills, so when I started throwing up, everyone thought I was carsick. Every morning I was throwing up, and all day I was throwing up in this very cold, stone place called Brackenhurst. I was so cold and so sick. Praise God that Cecil was able to take care of the older children. It was hard to enjoy that conference.

There's not much anyone can do when you have morning sickness. I remember, even when we had to come down the winding road to go to the airport after the conference, I thought I was going to throw up in the middle of the airport. Well, first I thought I was going to throw up in the middle of the jeep, and then I thought I was going to throw up in the middle of the airport. I finally did get to the bathroom before I threw up. Those are my wonderful memories of Kenya – far over-shadowing any sightings of lion, zebra, or antelope on other visits when I wasn't pregnant.

Marvelous Mauritius

Mauritius is a beautiful island in the Indian Ocean. We stopped there on our 1987 trip back to the U.S. Deborah was a baby. In southern Africa, there was a point when, if you lived in Zambia, you did your holidays in Zimbabwe, because Zimbabwe was at that time a very beautiful place to visit. If you lived in Zimbabwe, you did your holidays in South Africa. If you lived in South Africa, you did your holidays in Mauritius. (I guess the grass is always greener somewhere else!) Well, the word got back even to Zambia that Mauritius was a wonderful place to have a holiday. We had an opportunity to add a free stop in Mauritius to our furlough flight to the U.S., so we did. We had a tiny little cottage right on the beach in Mauritius. The waves weren't big at

all. It was all very calm. The children, even Deborah, could play safely at the edge of the crystal-clear water. A man came by every day on his bicycle selling yogurt. There was no yogurt in Zambia......no milk products at all, most of the time.......and certainly not yogurt. So that was fun. The bad part of this trip was that Cecil had malaria, but he didn't know he had malaria at the time. At the time, he just thought he had the flu. (It was not until we arrived in Kentucky that he tested for malaria).

He was so sick, throwing up all day every day. The roads in Mauritius were really wind-y in the mountains until you got down to the beach. Because of that, at first he thought he was carsick as a result of our taxi ride from the airport to the beach. Even before that, when he got off the plane, he thought he was airsick. Then he thought it was carsickness. He was just sick the whole time, so it wasn't very much fun. I had a baby, so I couldn't go out much. At least the children could play right outside the door on the beach. There was a restaurant way down on the beach that Cecil and the children could walk to when he felt like walking. There were also sights to see, but Cecil didn't feel like going anywhere, and I couldn't go alone. Even on the way back to the airport, Cecil had to take a bucket in case he needed to throw up in the taxi. So that was Mauritius – a lovely place to vacation if you don't have malaria.

Zany Zimbabwe

Zimbabwe, the former Southern Rhodesia, is the country south of Zambia. The borders were closed between Zambia and Zimbabwe when we first went to Zambia in 1976 because of civil war in Zimbabwe. The borders re-opened when independence was declared in 1980. After that point, we were allowed to cross the border into Zimbabwe. Well, we tried that. When we tried, however, there was a question on the immigration form that said, "Have you ever been convicted of a felony?" Cecil truthfully answered, "Yes." Oops! The Zimbabwean immigration officials did not like that answer. So, even though his criminal record had been purged because of the length of time between the offense and that year, we had great difficulty in entering Zimbabwe. Shame! That's where our southern Africa mission retreat was held. That's where any good doctors were, and eventually Cecil needed a good doctor because he had a fungus in his ear that was causing fluid build-up behind the eardrum and was making his life miserable. Any time we needed or desired to go to Zimbabwe, Cecil had to get special permission and then be fingerprinted at the border. Because of this, we missed several events that took place in Zimbabwe.

One of our first experiences in Zimbabwe was camping with Zambia Christian Mission missionaries and a few missionaries from Zimbabwe. We camped at Lake Kariba in tents. Hippos would come up out of the lake right beside our tent! I will never forget that.

During that trip, Cecil took Ben and the Davises' son, David, out on the lake to fish. While they were out in the boat, a storm came up. Lake Kariba, I am told, is like the Sea of Galilee, in that storms come up very suddenly. Cecil was unable to get the boat back to shore before dark fell and had to pull up to an island and spend the night. Of course, all of us at the camp were extremely worried. Ginger Conley spent most of the night waving a lantern, in case Cecil was trying to get to shore. I did not sleep. Early the next morning, Cecil and the boys rowed into shore. We were all very happy.

Once, I took the children across the border by myself into the town of Kariba. Cecil went as far as the game park in Zambia, and the rest of the family crossed over into Kariba to go shopping for the day. On another occasion, when Cecil had permission to cross, we stayed at a little resort called the Most High Hotel. That was fun. Missionaries ran the resort, and they gave special discounts – or, actually, we could stay free, if we couldn't afford to pay – or give a gift in whatever amount we could afford. On this particular occasion, there were elephants in the street in front of the resort. They chased the children! The children ran! They had to run, run, run. They ran to a house, but the door wouldn't open. Thankfully, the elephants continued along the paved road.

Another time, we were on the road from Zimbabwe back to Zambia, and there was an elephant in the middle of the road. He was there with his ears flapping. It was a great picture.

In the capital city of Harare, there was a Wimpy's fast food restaurant. I remember eating there on the way to a retreat at Rest Haven. What a treat to have a fast-food hamburger in those days!

At Rest Haven, we met missionaries from all over southern Africa. Those were great retreats, even though the weather was cold because the retreats were held in July. For that reason, most of my memories of Zimbabwe are of cold weather. That sounds strange for southern Africa, doesn't it?

Engaging Europe

Europe was sometimes a stopover on our trips to and from Zambia. Once we flew through England. At that time, I had a child with an ear infection. So while everybody else went out to see Big Ben and the palace guard, I stayed in a little room in London with a child with an ear infection. That's what I remember about England.

We flew into Belgium once but only got to see the airport. We flew into France on our first trip to Zambia – you have read that story already. You know the Germany story. We flew through Germany on another occasion as well. The Dutch doctor who had treated Deborah for meningitis was then living again in Holland while completing a course in tropical medicine. He had invited us to visit him on our way back to the U.S. He picked us up at the airport in Germany and then drove us to Holland. We spent several days at the place where he was living. It was called "The Friends." He had a little apartment for his family, but the rest of the place was a big dormitory-style situation. We had a room there and breakfast there. It was a place somewhat like a commune. We stayed at the commune and rented a car to drive into Belgium and France. Such beautiful countryside but horrendous traffic in the cities! Nobody got sick, and I was able to see everything the rest of the family saw. The children were growing up. Life was getting easier.

Not Namibia

By the end of 1990, fourteen years after arriving in Zambia, Cecil and I began to consider re-locating. We could see that there seemed to be some well-trained people, including the 12 men and their wives who had just completed three years of concentrated study at Musili Training Center, leading the churches in Zambia. Most of the churches were standing on their own. There had been missionaries in Zambia with Zambia Christian Mission since 1967. Twenty-three years later it seemed conceivable that we should look for another country where the need might be greater.

So we began praying and looking. We looked at Namibia because it was a newly-birthed country. After making a survey trip, we determined that Namibia seemed to be pretty well churched, at least in the capital city area. We deemed that we would have to live in a city for the educational sake of our children.

When we returned to Zambia, despite my fascination with the Herero women in their traditional dress, we did not feel that God was leading us to Namibia.

There is an interesting little sidebar to that story, though. One night while we were in Namibia, we went out for pizza. You would never believe whom we saw in that little tiny pizza place. It was Dr. Pete – the doctor who treated Deborah for meningitis, the doctor we visited in Holland! It had been at least three years since we'd seen him. At least three years, and there he was at that place in Namibia, miles and miles and miles and miles and miles away from Zambia. It really is a small world after all!

Mozambique It Was

Not long after the decision was made NOT to go to Namibia, Cecil was in contact with Jacob Michael. Jacob had been working in Zimbabwe for several years and had crossed the border into Mozambique on several occasions. Jacob invited Cecil to go on a survey trip with him to Mozambique. Cecil came back from the trip convinced that God was calling us to Mozambique. We returned to Kentucky in June, 1991, for furlough in order to report to the churches concerning the work in Zambia and begin making preparations to enter Mozambique.

At Lake James School of Missions the summer of 1991, Jon and Bonna Ray, "older" (the same age as we) students at Johnson Bible College, decided to throw in their hats as well, and Good News for Africa (in Portuguese, Boa Nova para Africa) was founded. As recorded in the minutes of the board of directors meeting on February 15, 1992, Cecil read a letter of resignation from Zambia Christian Mission. David Eubanks moved that the resignation be accepted with regret and deep appreciation for the Byrds' seventeen years of faithful service, saying, "Cecil and Betty have evidenced a deep love for the Zambian people and a steadfast commitment to the work. Although it is with sadness that the Board sees them leave Zambia, it is also with a sense of excitement and anticipation for the new work they will be pioneering in Mozambique. For that new venture the Board extends to the Byrds strong encouragement as well as their prayers for the direction, leading, and blessing of God." Denver Sizemore seconded the motion, which carried.

During the rest of the year, much work was put into incorporating this mission as a 501(c)3 in the state of Ohio. During this time, Cecil and I both returned to school – he through distance studies from Johnson Bible College and I as a full-time student at Spalding University in Louisville, Kentucky. In May, 1993, Cecil completed his M.A. in New Testament Preaching and Exposition, and I received an M.A. in Teaching and was certified in the Commonwealth of Kentucky to teach grades K-4 and self-contained grades 5 and 6. Six weeks after our graduations, we headed to Mozambique.

When we arrived in Maputo, the capital city of Mozambique, our house was not ready. In fact, it wasn't even started. We had been warned beforehand, but we could not stay in the U.S. any longer. We had already been in the mission house in Louisville for two years. It was time to move on so someone else could move in.

Jacob and Nila Michael met us at the airport in Maputo and took us to

the place they were staying temporarily, because their house wasn't finished yet, either. Jon Ray was building duplexes on seven hectares of land that had been given to Good News for Africa by an association of independent churches in Mozambique. This property was designated for use for mission purposes. Jon had finished the first half of the first duplex, and Bonna and he had moved in. Jon then started on the second half, which was Jacob and Nila Michael's house. They were already in Mozambique, but they had been renting a place from Henry Holmgren, a Baptist missionary who was on furlough. The Michaels' temporary housing was a very tiny, tiny place. When we arrived with three of our children, we had to sleep at their house with them in that little place. There weren't enough beds. So here we were, all squished into one room. The children had to sleep on the floor, and we were on a single bed, squished up together, but very thankful that the Michaels were willing to share Henry's house with us.

This was June, 1993. Kathy was 15, Daniel was 11, and Deborah was 7. We lived in this house with the Michaels for a few days, until the floor in the Michaels' duplex was dry enough to walk on. Then we moved into the Michaels' duplex, and they stayed on in Bro. Holmgren's house until our house was finished two months later. We began studying Portuguese, meeting the churches who had invited us to come to Mozambique, and I began teaching first grade at Trichardt School where our children were enrolled.

The first years in Mozambique were very hard years. Often there was no electricity and no water running to the house. I had to get up at 4:00 each morning to haul water from the bairro water spigot. There was not enough pressure to get water up to our house. Later, we built a storage tank to hold water that could be pumped to our houses. The men attached plastic storage tanks to the side of each house. We did not have hot water heaters; but during the summers, the water was warmed by the sun. It was just a bit chilly in the winter months. Later we were able to purchase heating elements to place in the plastic tanks. We could turn the elements on before showers to warm the water but needed to remember to turn the elements off afterward so as not to melt a hole in the tank. We only failed once! And, yes, it was my fault. Missionaries who came later to Mozambique were able to purchase "real" electric water heaters.

I remember each fruit tree and each strand of grass we planted (yes, we planted grass by strands, not seeds!) and all the flowers as well. What a beautiful flower garden I made. That dry, dusty piece of land took on life after some hard months and years of labor.

We, too, eventually became used to living there, but it was always hard compared to the years we lived and worked in Zambia.

Sweet Swaziland

Swaziland is a nice little country just across the border from Mozambique. Sometimes we went there to shop, and sometimes we went through Swaziland to get to South Africa. There was a Church of Christ Bible Institute in Swaziland. Manuel and Pam d'Oliveira taught at the Bible college in Swaziland. They eventually came to live and work with Good News for Africa in Mozambique. A couple of students from Mozambique were also trained in the college.

Succulent South Africa

South Africa is where we purchased anything that was ever worth purchasing. During our early years in Zambia, when the borders were closed to Zimbabwe, Cecil would go with friends through Botswana to go to South Africa. We bought vehicles there and sometimes Christmas presents. When we first lived in Mozambique, there was nothing of anything within the country to buy. We couldn't buy a vehicle there because the price and taxes were way too high. We bought a vehicle from a man in South Africa and kept his address on the title so that made it possible to drive it into Mozambique without importing the truck. Every 30 days we'd have to drive out because we were only allowed to keep foreign vehicles in the country for 30 days at a time. That was, however, convenient, because every 30 days we got to go back to South Africa to shop. That' where we did all of our grocery shopping. We would buy a month' worth of groceries at a time, get haircuts, see the doctor and orthodontist, eat fast food or in a restaurant, and see a movie in a theater. Cecil made friends with the butcher in Nelspruit, and sometimes we would go for tea or a braii (cookout) at his house.

The little town of Nelspruit, South Africa, where we shopped, was four hours away from Maputo over a very rough, potholed dirt road. Some of the potholes were more like craters than holes. We would have to creep along this road in the heat and the dust so as not to injure our vehicle or our backs. Now the South African government has made a beautiful, paved road between the two countries. I hear it now takes less than half the time to make the trip.

When we first moved to Mozambique in 1993, sixteen years of civil war within the country had just ended. The United Nations was still in the country to monitor the peace. They manned the road between Mozambique and South Africa as many robberies occurred along that road. For the first year or so, we only traveled the road in convoy as repeated ambushes took place when people had to slow down for potholes.

The trips to South Africa enabled us to escape the bush for a couple of days and regain our sanity in order to continue to work in Mozambique. I am so thankful for the medical help we received in South Africa as well--from Deborah's CT scan and shunt insertion in 1986 through a shunt revision in 1999. We would not have been able to stay in Zambia or Mozambique had it not been for the good medical facilities and care in South Africa.

Bophuthatswana

Our friends, Jim and Ginger Conley, eventually moved from Zambia to Bophuthatswana. We went to visit them there and got caught between the borders of Bophuthatswana and South Africa. By the time we got through the border in Bophuthatswana, the South African border had closed for the night. We were in no-man's land between borders and had to sleep in the truck.

The Cost of Going into All the World

The hardest part was going in the first place, but the cost of going into all the world was in the leaving. We had counted the cost of leaving mothers, fathers, brothers, sisters, houses, and lands, but we had not counted, nor even imagined, the cost of one day leaving our children in another part of the world.

Perhaps one of the best parts of living overseas was the raising of a large family in the wide, open spaces of the African continent. Those were happy days. Often when I think of the difference between living in Zambia and in Mozambique, I think about how much happier I was living in Zambia because that was when we were raising five children, and all of us lived in one place.

During our last three years in Zambia, our oldest son, Ben, graduated from high school. He returned to the U. S. to enter Johnson Bible College. He was excited to go; we were happy for him. We had no idea, however, what emotions such a separation could evoke. We were happy when Ben returned a year and a half later to finish out the last six months of our final years in Zambia.

The cost of leaving became even greater at the end of our furlough in 1993. That time, we were leaving both Ben and Miriam. Ben was deployed by the Marines on a ship at the time, and we didn't even get to say a face to face good-bye. Miriam, however, was standing the night we left in the drive-way of the mission house where we had lived during furlough. Three years later, that scene was repeated as we left our second daughter, Kathy, standing in that same driveway. Kathy later wrote about those times in the poem below. I still feel the pain each time I read it.

He Prayed
By Kathryn Elizabeth Byrd Willingham

The sun has already set
Though there are traces of it still
Everything is packed up
Suitcases are padlocked
The drawers and closets are empty
All of the sheets, blankets, and curtains
Have been taken down or pulled off
Washed and replaced
The carpet has been cleaned and there are no dirty dishes
Everything personal is gone
The house is now as it was

The van is ready to go
Loaded up with anything we could take with us
Pillows are placed in chosen seat
There are no more preparations to make
All has been returned
Good-byes to friends have already been taken care of
The gas tank is full
Stop stalling
It's time to go

But wait
I have to hug her one more time

I have to smell her and log it in my memory
Take a picture in my mind
Frame it in gold
Last words, let's be impressionable
Let's have something to hold

I heard him cry out
A man of great strength
As he wrapped his arms around his oldest daughter
And tears rolled freely down
He prayed
I turned from them, my pain too great

Years passed by
And then one evening
A scene passed through my head
Of a time not so long ago
My turn had come
I looked up to the sky
It was splashed with pinks and purple
My gaze was on the empty house
I turned and faced my father
He wrapped his arms about me
He prayed

Preach
The Word

Homiletics

Cecil's preaching career began at Johnson Bible College. He was never a boy preacher – far from it. His teenage days were far removed from the church, youth groups, preaching contests, etc. His first attempts at preaching came at Johnson Bible College when he studied homiletics under Dr. Gary Weedman, now president of Johnson University. My first birthday present to Cecil was *Strong's Concordance.* He was thrilled! I think that gift sealed our relationship.

On May 12, 1972, Cecil graduated from Johnson Bible College with a B.A. in Bible. In 1991, Cecil enrolled in the Johnson Bible College distance learning program and two years later was awarded an M.A. in New Testament Exposition and Preaching.

He loved studying the Word; he loved preaching the Word.

Bloomington

Cecil became acquainted with Bloomington Christian Church in Byrdstown, Tennessee, when Mike Sabens invited him to help out with the youth at both Bloomington and Byrdstown Christian churches during his freshman year at Johnson. When Mike graduated in May, 1970, he moved to Byrdstown to become the full-time minister at Byrdstown Christian. Cecil began preaching regularly on the weekends at Bloomington Christian Church. That meant a five hour drive every Saturday from Knoxville to Byrdstown. We would leave campus every Saturday after classes ended at noon, Cecil would preach on Sunday morning and Sunday evening, and then we would drive back to Knoxville. We were able to purchase a car for that journey in February of that year from an elder who owned a car dealership in Byrdstown. He allowed us to pay him $100 a month for the car. At the time, I was working full-time at Prudential Insurance Company in Knoxville, and Cecil was paid $100 per week as the preacher at Bloomington.

During Week of Evangelism at Johnson that year, Cecil and I drove to Bloomington for the weekend, and I drove the car back to Knoxville so that I could work. It was dark by the time I left Bloomington, and it was pouring down rain. I could only see the taillights of the truck in front of me as I made my way down that curvy mountain toward I-40. There was no place to pull off. It was just a narrow, winding road. I thought, "If I can get to the bottom of that mountain, I will just shoot straight across the highway and go to Spencer and Pat Garner's house and spend the rest of the night!" But somehow I missed the road to their house (still couldn't see because of the rain) and had to keep driving to Knoxville.

My eyes were so strained (I was wearing contact lenses) that the next day I couldn't open my eyes. There were very few people in the dorm because it was Week of Evangelism. There was one other couple at the other end of the dorm, so I just had to feel my way down the wall of the dorm and knock on their door. The wife took me to the eye doctor. He put some kind of drops in my eyes, and eventually I could open my eyes and see again. This doesn't have much to do with preaching the Word, but it's what happened to me because Cecil was preaching the Word!

The time we spent at Bloomington was a very good time. When we were married in December, 1969, Cecil was still working with the youth. The church was very good to us. They gave us a lovely shower, and two of the ladies gave us handmade quilts, the work of their very own hands.

Bloomington was the rural church, out in the country on the road to Star Point Boat Dock. It was a lovely church with lovely people. People always invited us home for Sunday dinner, for supper before church on Sunday evening, and for fellowship after the evening service. Those were very good days. We spent Saturday nights in a boarding house in Byrdstown or in the home of one of the Bloomington Christians. Those long, sleepy drives from Byrdstown back to Knoxville on Sunday nights/early Monday mornings were probably the longest periods of time we had alone before it was back to work, back to studying, and back to another weekend drive to Byrdstown.

A year later, when I became pregnant with our first child, we decided to give birth in Byrdstown rather than Knoxville. There was a doctor in the church at Bloomington, although only his wife attended church on a regular basis. Dr. Copeland was always busy with patients. At the end of the summer before the baby was due in October, we rented a trailer near the Bloomington church. The plan was that by the first week of October, I would stay in the trailer in Byrdstown until after the baby was born. Cecil would continue to travel back and forth between Knoxville and Byrdstown on the weekends.

A couple of weekends after we rented the trailer, our world at Bloomington fell apart. Cecil asked one of the elders at Bloomington to pray, and the elder refused. Cecil couldn't believe that an elder wouldn't pray. He walked out of the church. He said he wasn't going to preach in a church where elders wouldn't pray. Well, that's OK, but I was just about to have a baby. That made a big problem.

The elder was a very good man — just shy of praying in public. Cecil, of course, being very young in ministry, acted much too impulsively in this situation. We went back to the trailer, packed up everything that we had just moved down there, and took it all back to Knoxville.

Eventually, there was healing. The church contacted the school, and the academic dean, Dr. Clark, had a talk with Cecil. They went back to the church, and Cecil apologized for his impulsiveness and bad behavior. The church asked him to please come back. They were upset that he wasn't the preacher, anymore. They loved him so much. I think they loved me, too, but they really loved him more, and they wanted him to be the preacher. There was reconciliation, but Dr. Clark advised him not to go back.

The relationship with Bloomington did not end. We went back there to preach revivals and to help with vacation Bible schools. When we decided to go to Zambia as missionaries, they were one of our $100 a month supporters for years and years and years. Every home service, Cecil went back there to preach, to hunt, and to fish. The doctor's wife, who owned Star Point Boat Dock and Restaurant, gave us an acre of land on the lake. We planned to build a log cabin and retire there. On every visit, she invited us to stay in the cottages and use the pontoon boats and fishing boats. After Cecil died, however, I sold the land for $10,000 and used the money as part of the down payment for the house I live in now.

Thank you, Bloomington, for such precious memories! Cecil couldn't have asked for a better place to begin preaching the Word.

Woodlawn

After Cecil left Bloomington, he began preaching at Woodlawn Christian Church in Campbellsville, Kentucky. He was then a first semester senior at Johnson and nearly to become a father. Because I was so near to giving birth, I did not travel with him to Campbellsville on the weekends. It was not until after Ben was born that I was able to make the trip for the first time. Cecil was uneasy leaving me alone in our little cottage on the French Broad River, so I had to stay with the basketball coach, Russell Morgan, and his wife, Jean.

For our entire senior year in college (I finished my last class during Cecil's last semester), we traveled every weekend to Campbellsville. Then May 12, 1972, finally arrived, and we graduated from Johnson Bible College. The next day, some people from Campbellsville came with a pick-up truck, and we loaded into it the crib, the rocking chair, and the toy chest (that's all the furniture we owned!) along with a few dishes and some pots and pans. Everything fit in that pickup truck, and we moved to Campbellsville and into the parsonage of Woodlawn Christian Church.

Our Sunday school class at Woodlawn gave us money to buy a bedroom suite. The maple double bed, dresser, and chest of drawers cost a total of $350. The church gave us money to buy a couch and a chair in the living room, and then I had a rocking chair in Ben's room. A lady loaned us her cherry coffee table. There was a big vacant lot beside the parsonage. We planted a garden there in the summer. In the back yard, there was a garage. Cecil built a pen beside the garage and bought beagles as hunting dogs.

Cecil preached on Sunday mornings and Wednesday evenings. He visited people in the hospital when they were sick and the shut-ins on a regular basis. Otherwise, it was not a very demanding job. He visited a lot of the church members and built strong relationships. I was alone a lot with Baby Ben while Cecil was out visiting and building relationship. For the first time ever, I found my daily routine slightly boring. I had very little furniture to dust. The house was easy to take care of. Cecil usually had the car because he was always visiting someone, so it wasn't like I could go anywhere. Once a week, I would go to the grocery store, and he would keep the baby. I actually asked at one point, "Can I get a job?" Ben was such a good sleeper. He would sleep until 9 in the

morning. He would go back for a nap at 1 and sleep until 5 in the afternoon, and then go back to bed at 7 or 8. He was an easy baby to take care of.

Cecil did not want me to have a job, however, even when one of the church members offered me the job of activity director at a nursing home. He wanted me to be at home to take care of the house and the baby. I read a lot and even started watching soap operas.

Almost all of the women in the church worked. My roommate from college lived in Campbellsville, but she worked, too. I became friends with her sister, Ivana, and she convinced me to join the local Homemakers Club. So now, I bought groceries once a week, went to Homemakers once a month, to Women's Fellowship at church once a month, Sunday school and church on Sunday mornings and evening, and church on Wednesday evenings.

At Homemakers, I had to make a crazy quilt and a Carnation dessert. Somehow, I got elected president of the Homemakers Club, but I don't know why as I was most unqualified as a homemaker. So, when Al Hamilton proposed that we should go as missionaries to Papua New Guinea, I thought, "That's how I can get out of being the president of the Homemakers Club! Let's go!" I put up no resistance whatsoever to the suggestion. I said, "Let's go!" For me, going to Papua New Guinea would be so much easier than being the president of the Taylor County Homemakers Club. In fact, it would be the beginning of the dream I had dreamed since high school – just actualized in a different part of the world. This happened in May of 1974.

Two years after moving to Campbellsville, Al Hamilton came to Woodlawn in an attempt to recruit people to join a new organization, Pioneer Bible Translators. Cecil had asked the church early in his ministry to pray that God would raise up someone from Woodlawn to go as a missionary to an unreached part of the world. When Al preached, Cecil and I became the answers to the prayer the church had been praying.

The church was not happy that we were leaving. They said, "We don't want you to go. What are we going to do? We've been really good to you." This caused us to feel uneasy. We called Max Ward Randall, who had served as a missionary and was then on the board of directors for Zambia Christian Mission. He said, "If God is calling you, then you have to go."

In a very short time, two weeks or less, we had packed up everything into a tiny U-Haul trailer. "Everything" consisted of Ben's crib and toy box, a few books, and our clothes. We sold our bedroom set and gave our living room furniture to the very Al Hamilton who had asked us to go. With the U-Haul trailer attached to our blue Gran Torino, we headed off to Norman, Oklahoma, to begin classes at the Summer Institute of Linguistics at the University of Oklahoma.

Cecil believed he could exchange a preaching vocation for a Bible translation ministry.

Bella Vista

After finishing the summer course at Norman, we moved to Dallas for further training at the International Linguistics Center. While we were in Dallas, Cecil began an interim weekend ministry at Bella Vista Christian Church in Garland, Texas. The salary he received from this ministry was a great help in paying the hospital for the delivery of our second child, Miriam. Cecil continued to minister at Bella Vista until we finished our training in May. The Bella Vista church continued to support us after we left Dallas, becoming one of our first supporters in missions work. Two families from that church became supporters as well. Even though the Bella Vista church no longer exists, those two families continue to support missions through their gifts to the account that I manage through Team Expansion.

Make

Disciples

There are some people I will never forget. Here's just a sprinkling of a few followers of Jesus we met or made along the way.

Ba Matyoka

Before we arrived in Zambia, Ba Mutyoka was chosen by the previous missionaries and the church leaders in Ndola to take the position of evangelist among the eight established churches. The missionaries bought him a motorcycle so that he would have transportation to those churches. He was very helpful to us in the beginning of our ministry in Zambia since we didn't speak the language and we didn't know where the churches were located.

Ba Mutyoka became Cecil's best friend and traveling companion as they made their way among the churches on their motorcycles. Eventually, as with all people who succumb to the temptation for power, an issue of pride became apparent. Ba Mutyoka fell away and was removed from that leadership role.

Ba William Lazalo

Ba Lazalo was the righteous, Godly leader of the Lubuto (which means light in Bemba and Lamba) Church of Christ, a church which was already established when we arrived in Zambia. In the beginning of our ministry, Ba Lazalo was a man from whom we could seek advice and counsel concerning traditions, practices, and culture. His wife, Ba Judith, was a leader among the women of Zambia and was often at the forefront of organizing women's conferences and praying with women who were demon-possessed.

Ba Henry

Ba Henry was the leader of the Ndeke church in Ndeke Township. Ndeke means airport, and this township was so named because it was located near the airport. Ba Henry was a cordial and hospitable man (having at least 14 extended family members living in his small cinder block house). He was discipled by the Davises and Delaneys and continued to thrive in the years we worked in Ndola. Ba Henry worked hard in the Ndeke church on weekends and evenings when he came home from his banking job in the city each day.

Ba Jenipher Musinkanye

Ba Jenipher was one of the fruits of the work in Ndeke Township. When we first visited the Ndeke church, Ba Jenipher was a young girl. She told us later that when we came that day to church, we were the first white people that she had ever seen, and she was very afraid of us. She actually left the church building and ran back home. As she grew up, Jenipher came to know the missionaries very well. In 1977, Gary and Meta Burlington came to live in Ndola and worked alongside of us. At that point, Gary and Meta continued the work in the township churches of Lubuto, Ndeke, and Kawama, while we continued to work with the rural churches. Ba Jenipher got to know the Burlingtons very well. By the time the Burlingtons arrived, she was no longer afraid of white people. By the time she was a teenager, the Burlingtons had moved north to Kasama, and Jenipher attached herself to us. She visited us frequently, usually on her way home from school. After finishing secondary school, Jenipher went away to a home economics school run by the Catholic church. She was already gifted in sewing and in all kinds of needlework and handwork. She picked up more skills in cooking and nutrition as she completed the Domestics course that the school offered..

A few years later, when we started the training school for leaders in Musili village, Jenipher was ready and eager to share what she had learned with the leaders' wives. She worked with me to help in the women's work. She was a great help with all of the domestics classes. Jenipher was able to help the ladies design patterns for children's clothes and for themselves, as well as teach them to sew by hand, embroider, crochet, and knit.

Ba Jenipher and I worked together to help the women with a soybean project in order to improve nutrition, especially for their children. The twelve ladies at the training center planted a field of soybeans. While the soybeans were growing, Jenipher taught the ladies how to build a clay oven. Once the soybeans were harvested, the ladies learned from Jenipher how to prepare the soybeans so that their children could benefit from the extra protein. We roasted and salted soybeans and ate them like peanuts as snacks. We boiled and mashed soybeans and made all kinds of breads and cookies in the clay oven and in the frying pan. We even made a soybean spread for sandwiches.

Ba Jenipher continued to work diligently during all of the three years that the training center in Musili was in existence. When we left Zambia the next year, Jenipher continued as much as possible working with women in the villages and townships and in the prisons. Her work in the villages and townships was somewhat hindered, however, because she never married, which was somewhat of a taboo in the culture.

Jenipher and I also began a Bible club for teenaged girls who attended the English-speaking church in town. .We gathered on Sunday afternoons to study the Bible and play games. Jenipher helped the girls learn to sew, make baby clothes, teddy bears, and other stuffed animals. On occasion, we would visit the old people in the nursing home. Jenipher continued the work with the girls' club after we left Zambia.

During those years, every Sunday Jenipher would come home with us after English church, have lunch with us, and visit until time for the Girls Bible Club. One day Jenipher said to me, "Bana Miriam, you have taught me many things from the Bible, but I learned the most about living a Christian life by being with you in your home. I saw how you treated your husband and how your raised your children. Now I know how to live as a Christian."

Eventually, Jenipher's parents moved back to the Northern Province, leaving only Jenipher and three or four of her brothers and sisters still living in Ndeke.

Jenipher was sick a lot. She had hemophilia and had to get blood transfusions frequently. At that time, we didn't know how harmful that was. Those years when Jenipher was receiving blood were the beginning of the age of AIDS, a time when blood was not screened in Zambia.

Jenipher contracted AIDS from the transfusions and went to live with her parents in the Northern Province where she died. If I could etch her tombstone, it would read, "Dedicated Disciple of Our Lord, Jesus Christ."

Clodie (Claudette) Ross

Clodie was a little girl of mixed race who lived across the wall from us in Ndola when we lived at 16 Kuomboka Crescent. My daughter, Miriam, and Clodie were friends. Miriam and Clodie would sit on the wall between our two yards and on top of the ant hill and exchange stories and catch flying ants. When it rained, all of the children would slide down the slick, red clay of the ant hill, pretending it was a slide. Then they would have to be hosed off before they could come into the house.

Clodie and Miriam converted our rabbit hutch into a little playhouse. They scrubbed it and scoured it and brought in odd pieces of furniture and a charcoal brazier. They made tea and porridge on the brazier, just like Ben and his friend Francis had done a few years before. Clodie was frequently in our house but never attended church with us as her family was Catholic. We left Zambia in 1991 when Miriam and Clodie were both sixteen.

Seven years later, while Cecil and I were still in Mozambique, Clodie, then a young woman in a professional position, obtained our address from someone in Ndola. She wrote to say thank you for showing her Jesus. It was evident that she, too, had become a disciple of Christ.

Ba Michael Singano

Ba Michael Singano helped to start and became a leader of the Musili Church of Christ. He became a strong Christian and was very, very helpful in the ministry.

Ba Michael was instrumental in making it possible to start a training center in the village at Musili where we built 12 mud huts to which families (all followers of Christ) from 12 different villages moved to engage in three years of training. Ba Michael was a good friend to Cecil and helped him in many ways.

Frikkie Botha

Frikkie was the butcher who helped us with meat from his butchery when we crossed the border into South Africa every month. Cecil and Frikkie became very good friends, and Cecil frequently talked to him about Christ. Of course, being South African, he had somewhat of a Christian background in the Dutch Reformed Church, but he was not a practicing Christian. We had many braais – barbecues – at his house and spent many evenings talking about Jesus. He now attends church faithfully and loves the Lord.

Lawrence and Martha Temfwe

Cecil began going into the prisons in Zambia because of an association with a wealthy businessman who had served time in prison. When he was released from prison several months later, he began a prison ministry in which Cecil became involved. He and Cecil worked to incorporate the ministry through Prison Fellowship International.

During one of his visits to Kamfinsa Prison in Ndola, Cecil met Lawrence Temfwe. Lawrence became a Christian while in prison. When he was released, Cecil continued to disciple him. Lawrence was very instrumental in helping Ross and Chris Logan start the English-speaking church in Ndola. After we left Zambia, Lawrence came to the U.S., went to Wheaton College, and is presently involved in a very effective ministry in Zambia. My daughter, Miriam, and her family were able to participate in this ministry with Lawrence and his wife during the summer of 2011.

Lawrence met Martha, a young woman in one of the local churches. Lawrence asked Cecil to perform a marriage ceremony for them. Lawrence and Martha's wedding was a Western-style wedding. Martha wore a traditional white wedding gown, and our twelve year-old daughter, Miriam, played the piano for their wedding. Lawrence and Martha continue to be a good example of a Zambian Christian couple raising a Christian family (four children, all doing well) while ministering among the Zambian people.

Ba Stanley Malasya

Ba Stanley Malasya was a leader at the church in Makubi. He and his wife were one of the families who studied at the training center at Musili. Ba Stanley was a very faithful person and committed to his life as a Christian, which is not an easy thing within a culture entrenched in witchcraft.

Ba Daniel and Bana Daniel

Ba Daniel was another faithful leader at the Makubi church. He and his wife also studied at Musili Training Center. His wife, unlike the other wives studying at the center, had completed seventh grade in school and could speak

English well. Most of the other women could not read or write and spoke only the local languages.

Bana Daniel was a wonderful helper. While Jenipher was a great helper in the domestics training, the cooking, and sewing skills, Bana Daniel was a great helper when I needed an interpreter. She was also knowledgeable in the Bible. She was also a great help in teaching the other women to read and write through a book designed by Literacy International.

Ba William Chabala

Ba William was a leader from the Munkulungwe church. He was a little, bitty guy. He and his wife left their village to study at Musili Training Center for three years. During that time we were receiving used clothes from the U.S. I remember when one shipment arrived, and the people were going through the clothes to see what they wanted. Ba William came away with a woman's bathrobe, which he wore throughout the winter round about the compound.

Ba William's wife was one of the ladies whom I taught to read through a literacy course at Musili. After the training center closed, Cecil met Ba William's wife and Ba Stanley's wife on the road one day. They flagged him down on the road and he asked, "Do you want me to take you to your homes?" And they said, "No, we just want you to tell your wife, Bana Benjamin, how much our lives have changed since we learned how to read the Word of God."

Ba Gideon Phiri

Ba Gideon Phiri was also from Munkulungwe and also helped with the Kamboa church. He and his wife studied for three years at the Musili Training Center. After finishing his training at Musili, Ba Gideon began working in the area prisons and now serves as a prison chaplain.

When Miriam and her family visited Zambia in 2011, the churches in the villages of Munkulungwe, Kamboa, and Makubi came together for a one-day seminar to fellowship and learn from their visitors. The Malasyas, the Chabalas, the Phiris, and Ba Daniel and his family are all continuing to serve faithfully as disciples who are making more disciples.

Baptizing
Them

Zambia's Baptistries, Ponds, and Rivers

One of the strangest, funniest, grossest baptisms I ever saw was at the Chibwabwa (meaning "cabbage leaf") church. Of course, the baptism didn't occur in the church building, as there was no baptistry. These baptisms took place on a very hot Sunday afternoon. The sun had been beating down on the metal roof of the church building for several hours as we sat during the service. Then we walked in the scorching heat to a body of water. I guess you would call it a pond. We walked and we walked and we walked to get there. Of course, I had a baby tied to my back in the traditional Zambian way, so she added to the weight and the heat of the walk. When we finally got to the body of water, the preacher (Ba John) began to immerse the baptismal candidates. Each one came up out of the water covered in leeches! When they were once again on dry land, their friends and families gathered around to pull the leeches off of them.

The township churches, like Lubuto, Ndeke, and Kawama, all had baptistries in the church buildings. They were built just above the floor and covered with a piece of wood that could be removed when a baptism was to take place. The big advantage to these was that there were no leeches, and you didn't have to trek for miles to get to a body of water!

Cecil's 1986 summary report for Zambia Christian Mission indicates that, in that year alone, 300 people were baptized in the 32 churches in which we

worked within a 50 mile radius of Ndola. Multiply that number by 16 years and you will have an approximate idea of the number of people baptized from 1976-1991 as the number of churches grew from eight to forty.

Compound Baptistry and Indian Ocean in Mozambique

In Mozambique, we were far from a body of water as well. You would think we were close, because it looks like on the map that we were sitting on the Indian Ocean, but the distance was more than 16 kilometers to the bay. Since we didn't want to walk all of those kilometers every time (or even one time) someone wanted to be baptized, we built a baptistry outside of the building where we met for church on the Good News for Africa compound. This baptistry was made of cinder block. When someone wanted to be baptized, we would fill the baptistry with water from a hose pipe. When it wasn't in use, we would drain the water and put a cement cover on top so that children would not play (or drown) in it. Before the baptistry was built, we would have to pile people in the pickup truck and take them to the beach for baptisms.

Deborah was baptized at the age of nine while we were in Mozambique. We took her to the Indian Ocean to be baptized. That was quite an experience, too, because usually on the bay, which surrounded the city, the water always seemed very calm. On the day of Deborah's baptism, however, it looked like we might as well have been in the middle of the Atlantic Ocean. The waves were just rolling and the tide was just pulling. It took both Cecil and me to hold on to her so that she could be immersed and not drown in the process.

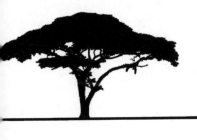

Teaching Them

Leadership Training by Extension

When we first arrived in Zambia, Cecil trained church leaders through a method known as leadership training by extension. He traveled weekly to each church to conduct classes with the men. As the churches grew in number, it was no longer possible to meet with each church weekly. Cecil began to gather leaders from three or four churches in close vicinity to one location so that the men could still learn on a weekly basis. The leaders of these churches were very dedicated and eager to learn. They were willing – even desired -- to sit in classes from early morning until the dark of night. They didn't want to take days off, either. If Christmas fell on their class day, they insisted on having class. They never wanted to cancel class.

Literacy Training and Women's Work

Eventually I had a car and could join Cecil in the afternoons once Ben was home from school. While he would teach the men inside the church building, I would teach the women outside under the trees in villages like Chibwabwa, Chiwala, Chisengi, Makubi, Munkulungwe, and Musili. All of the women wanted to learn to read so they could study the Bible on their own. I was able to obtain the government adult literacy materials, and we delved into learning to read and into making quilts and into studying God's Word. One of their favorite courses was "The Christian Family."

Musili Training Center

During the 1980's, some of the leaders were asking for more in-depth training. They wanted to have more than one day a week to learn the Word of God. They came up with a plan to build a small training center in the village of Musili. From 12 rural churches that were now established, one family from each church was chosen to go and build their own house and to study for a three-year period of time. We called the place where they studied Musili Training Center. The men took classes similar to those in Bible college, but not on the same level, since most of them only had a 7th grade education. Cecil would go to Musili for the whole day and half the evening every day to teach the men.

I was able to teach the women every morning after dropping my own children at school. By then I had my own car. Sometimes I would go back to town

to pick up the children from school and head back to Musili for the rest of the afternoon. A highlight of the three years at Musili for most of the women was learning to read. Of course, they loved the Bible, English, sewing, nutrition, and cooking classes, too. A favorite of both men and women was a study concerning how to live as a Christian family. You could see the families there really growing in maturity and in knowledge and in Christian living. The plan was to equip them to return to their own villages. And they did, even on weekends while they were still in training. They were not so far removed that they couldn't go back to their village churches. This class of 24 students graduated in December, 1990, after three years of study. All returned to minister in their home villages, and Ba Gideon Phiri became a prison chaplain through Prison Fellowship International.

The center closed after this class graduated.

Good News for Africa Training Center

We were invited to Mozambique by a group of 40 Zionist churches under an association called ACCIM (Association of Christian Churches in Mozambique). This association gave us seven hectares of land on which we were allowed to build houses. We also built a multipurpose building with a very large meeting room and small classrooms on the side. This building was eventually used as a church building as well and became the primary facility of the training center that was established on the compound. In the beginning, men from the area came to the center for evening classes, as many of them worked during the day. In the third year at the compound, a dormitory was built. This allowed men from the northern part of Mozambique to come down to the Boa Nova training center and live for several months at a time in order to take classes. A three-year program was established for these men. The first graduation at the center was held in December, 1999. That was a really big day – a really, really big day. Lots of celebrations. Lots of food, lots of cooking. The Minister of Justice came out for the ceremony. He was over education and religion in Mozambique.

Twelve students graduated on that grand day. A few days later, they returned to their homes in the provinces to the north – faithful men ready to commit what they had learned to other faithful men.

One month later, Cecil was killed. How wonderful that God allowed Cecil to see a conclusion to part of the vision he had had for Mozambique!

Trichardt School for Christian Education

Before we left Zambia, we were praying about where God would want us to go next. Cecil made a survey trip to Mozambique. During that survey trip, Cecil and Jacob Michael searched out opportunities for education in Mozambique. One of the schools they visited was the American school in Maputo. The director of the school said if I could get my teaching certification, then he would have a job for me. Our children then could go to school there for free. We would not be able to afford this very expensive school ($5,000 per year per child in 1993) otherwise.

When we returned to the U.S. for a two year transition period/educational furlough, Cecil pursued an M.A. in New Testament Exposition and Preaching, and I studied for a Master of Arts in Teaching for grades K-4 and self-contained 5 and 6.

When we arrived in Mozambique in June, 1993, we immediately checked on the job for me at the American school for the coming school year. The school director to whom Cecil had spoken in 1991 had moved on to other places, and the current director said, "We don't have any openings right now."

So then I felt like, "Oh my goodness-- two years I've spent getting my degree for this very reason, and now there are no openings." We soon learned, however, that a new school, Trichardt School for Christian Education, run by South Africans, had just opened six months earlier. A number of South African people were moving to Mozambique now that a peace treaty, ending civil war within the borders of Mozambique, had been signed. They started companies and pursued other development opportunities. This created a need for an English-medium school which their children could attend. Otherwise, they would have to learn Portuguese in order to attend the government schools in Mozambique. The school was started in January, 1993, but it had had problems during the first six months. Several teachers left, and children were withdrawn from the school. We arrived in June one week before the start of the next term of school with a new director, principal, and staff. There were still openings on staff, and I was hired to teach first grade. I had never wanted to teach first grade, preferring to have someone else responsible for laying such important groundwork in a child's education (first grade, or grade one as it is referred to in South Africa, was the first year of formal learning for South African children at that time). I gladly took the job, however, so that Kathy, Daniel, and Deborah could go to an English-medium school for no tuition. I also received $500 per month in renumeration. This was not the salary I would have received at the American school! From July 1, 1993-January 19, 2000, I taught at Trichardt School for Christian Education, except for furlough years from 1995-1996 and from April, 1998 through July, 1999.

The first year was hard, because I began teaching on July 1, 1993, one week after entering the country, in the middle of the school year, and not knowing any Portuguese. Three of the children in my class that year only spoke Portuguese; but Chantelle, who spoke both English and Portuguese, was a fairly willing interpreter. It helped that I only had four students: Chantelle, Dercio, Katia, and Nalia. It also helped that, even though the pay was low and the hours were long, the directors and principal were all Christians. It was wonderful to be able to teach Bible to these children every day. They were very receptive.

With the disbandment of the school in early 1993, there was a huge loss of equipment and books, so that made for an even rougher start in my teaching career. We made it through, though. Chantelle was withdrawn before the end of the year, Katia left in late November for Bulgaria, but we gained Nuno before her departure. So on December 15, 1993, the last day of school for that school year, Nuno, Nalia, and I sang "Little Donkey" in the Christmas Concert. Dercio didn't show.

I began my first full year of teaching in January, 1994, with sixteen students. Class size grew during the year to twenty. I was excited to go to school every day, and I enjoyed planning and preparing for the classes. I loved the students: Ibraimo from Portugal, Christopher from the U. S., Alexandre from Portugal/Mexico, Omoji from Nigeria, Urvi from Portugal/India, Cuthbert, Tumaini, John, Mashingia, and Leny from Tanzania, Adarsh and Harshna from India, Leigh from Swaziland/England, Kabwe and Jessy from Zambia, Priscila from Brazil, Hiwote from Ethiopia, Oswaldo from South Africa, Jean-Paul from Zaire, and Turi from Mozambique. The classroom was extremely crowded, but we did have some books and materials with which to work. Most of the children spoke English at least at some level.

How did all these kids from so many places end up in Mozambique in my classroom? Many of the third-world embassies sent their kids to Trichardt as did some serving with the U.N. and others who were part of foreign companies established in the country. Bible was part of the daily curriculum. I often felt like I was teaching ambassadors who would one day go back to their own countries and share the Good News they had learned at Trichardt. It was so cool – much better than teaching at a fancy American school where I would not have been allowed to teach Bible or sing songs about Jesus. I loved teaching at Trichardt. My only regret is that it kept me from involvement with the local people, especially teaching Mozambican women.

"In his heart a man plans his course, but the Lord determines his steps." Proverbs 16:9

"Many are the plans in a man's heart, but the Lord's purpose prevails." Proverbs 19:21

"A man's steps are directed by the Lord. How then can anyone understand his own way?" Proverbs 20:24

I believe the Lord determined to put me in touch with these students at Trichardt when all the while I thought I was preparing to teach at an elite American school.

Let me tell you a bit about some of the students at Trichardt:

Christopher was a U. S. citizen. His father was Haitian and worked far away in Nampula Province, and his American mother worked for the U.N. in Maputo. Christopher spent a great deal of his out-of-school hours with maids watching videos. He always wanted to talk about the movies he had seen. He especially liked cartoons.

Jean-Paul's parents were both Zairean. His father worked for U.S. Aid. Jean-Paul, the youngest of several children, was born in the U. S. while his father was studying at Tulane University.

Cuthbert, the youngest child of a Lutheran minister, was a tiny, bright Tanzanian boy with a squeaky, high-pitched voice. He had something to say about every subject discussed. He spun yarns in class for days about his new baby brother that didn't exist. He also told a whopping tale one day about not finishing his work in pre-school and having to go home with his teacher. His escape from her house during the night was even more fantastic. At the end of one particular day, Cuthbert exclaimed, "Oh, no, Miss Betty, we forgot to do reading today!"

"Oh, but we did do reading today, Cuthbert," I replied. "We didn't use our reading books; but remember the game we played with the letters of the alphabet – how we matched the capital letters to the lower-case letters and talked about the names and sound of all the letters? The alphabet is very important to reading. Without the alphabet, we couldn't make words; and without words, there would be nothing to read."

Then Cuthbert, who had just completed the Level 1 reader, In the Beginning, excitedly proclaimed, "Ms. Betty, I'm sooooooo thankful God created the alphabet so that we could learn to read!"

A little later in the year, Cuthbert made my day. I had often wondered how really effective I had been in teaching the children to read phonetically. On that day, we got out our new readers and were reading through as an overview – without introducing new words. On Cuthbert's page was the new word "castle". When he hesitated at the word, I immediately told him what it was – thinking it was far too difficult for him to sound out.

When I told him, he asked, "Are you sure, Miss Betty? It looks like cas –tle to me." I was so happy!

Every time I took my glasses off to clean them, Cuthbert told me how beautiful I was without them. Every teacher needs a Cuthbert in her class.

John was a little Tanzanian boy with very big glasses--so cute.

After greeting my class one morning, I was surprised to hear John gush, "Miss Betty, you look so nice today!"

Everyone else oohed and ahhed in agreement.

Since I looked no different to myself than any other day, I inquired curiously, "What is it that makes me look so nice today?"

"Is it my clothes? Is it my hair?" I inquired.

No, it's your BEAUTIFUL smile, Cuthbert the class spokesman replied.

"Well, I can't always wear nice clothes or have pretty hair, but I can always smile," I promised.

Educating Missionary Kids

Ben started first grade at age five (the British age to start school) at Kansenshi Primary, a local Zambian school. Ben and Ashu Sagar, the youngest of four little Indian boys who lived next door, left for school each morning in Mr. Sagar's Fiat. Mr. Sagar taught at Kansenshi Secondary School, so he conveniently dropped the two boys at Kansenshi Primary School on his way to work.

Missionaries who lived in Ndola years before had sent their children to Kansenshi, where they received an adequate education. In the few years that had passed, the quality of education had deteriorated. The schools once run by British expatriates had been Zambianized during the ten years since independence. Funding from outside sources had declined, and the schools were now over-crowded and understaffed. In Ben's first grade class, there were sixty students, fewer desks, one teacher (Mrs. Walubita), and plenty of chaos. I began volunteering to help with reading in that class.

Ben was the only Caucasian child in his classroom. There were two other Caucasians (a brother and sister from Zimbabwe) in the school, but not in Ben's class.

As the only Caucasian, Ben was very popular. He was never left alone. All the kids would follow him to the bathroom. Everywhere we went in that part of town, children were always hollering, "Ben-ja! Ben-ja! Ben-ja!"

By the end of that year, several expatriate companies had gotten together to form a company school, Nsansa, which means "happiness" in the Bemba language.

Ben started second grade in January, 1978, at Nsansa, where he was a student through sixth grade. He was followed there by his sisters and his brother. To us, Nsansa was, indeed, happiness; but it cost a lot of money. The ensuing school years meant I had to sell my sewing machine, have yard sales, and dream up other ways to finance private school educations.

We came home on furlough in time for Ben to do seventh grade at Christian Academy of Louisville. After that year, we returned to Zambia, and Ben was off to Rift Valley Academy, near Nairobi, Kenya, for eighth grade. He only got to come home at Christmas during the school year. So we saw him at Christmas and then in the summer.

Some have asked, "Did he like it?" To answer that question, I will have to express what I have learned about missionary kids since that time, something I wish that I had known years and years earlier.

Ben did not appear to be unhappy, but I now think that he was not that happy. Like many missionary kids, however, he would not have wanted to say anything that would upset what his parents were called to do. To make matters worse, he had been issued a back brace the summer before he entered Rift Valley. It seems that the boys in the dorm had quite a good time making fun of that back brace.

And yes, I think he was homesick. When he returned for ninth grade, I was pregnant with Deborah. When he came home for Christmas, he asked to let him come home for her birth. Then I knew he was missing his family.

In the end, he did come home and stay home, and we began a period of home-schooling. I was certainly glad to have him back in the same country, and he became the first and the last child we sent to boarding school.

In those days, in that part of Africa, lots of people sent their kids to boarding school. Good educational options were few and far between. Home-schooling had not come to the forefront. Boarding school often seemed to be the best educational option.

When parents expressed how difficult it was to do that, it was like, "OK, if you don't do that, you don't have any faith. Where is your faith that God will take care of your children? Hannah sent Samuel off to live with Eli, didn't he? What kind of people are you if you put your family before God?"

My conclusion on that matter is that kind of thinking is all hogwash. Wish I hadn't had to learn it the hard way.

So Ben finished out ninth grade by homeschooling through the University of Nebraska. We were in the U.S. for his sophomore year at Southern High School in Louisville, KY, and then back in Zambia with correspondence courses from the University of Nebraska at Lincoln to finish out eleventh and twelfth grades in record time. The following year, he entered Johnson Bible College, where he studied for a year and a half before re-joining us for our last six months in Zambia and then the U.S. Marine Corps. He completed his B.A. through Northwood University and has only a couple more classes to go to complete for his M.A. from Webster University

Miriam began kindergarten at Campbellsville Elementary School in Campbellsville, Kentucky, during our first furlough from Zambia in 1978. She was not yet five when school began, but she tested ready and was allowed to enter. Her teacher was Miss Mary Martin, a very special lady. She came to visitation in Louisville for Cecil's funeral 22 years later.

When we returned to Zambia, Miriam entered Nsansa School. I remember the school productions – especially the one in which Miriam was an angel. Her teacher was disappointed because we cut her long, blonde hair before the play. I also remember Miriam playing the piano for some of the school plays. She took lessons in Zambia from a Lutheran missionary and did quite well, earning excellent scores from the Royal School of Music. Miriam did fourth grade during our furlough in 1987 at Christian Academy of Louisville, went back to Nsansa for grades 5 and 6 and seventh grade at Christian Academy of Louisville, all that year longing to return to Zambia. When we returned to Zambia, Miriam home-schooled for ninth grade, entered a new private school in tenth grade, and completed her senior year in high school in Louisville during a furlough year. Miriam attended Sullivan University in Louisville, studying to be a travel agent, but married before finishing her degree. She is now attending Indiana Wesleyan, working on a degree in criminal justice.

Kathy went to reception class at Nsansa School and did first grade at Christian Academy of Louisville. She went to Nsansa for grades 2 and 3 and back to Christian Academy for grade 4. She attended Ndola Trust School for grades 5 and 6 and was home-schooled for grade 7. Kathy attended Bruce Middle School in Louisville for grade 8 and Southern High School for grade 9. She did the next two years of high school at Trichardt School for Christian Education in Mozambique and finished her senior year at Southern High School in Louisville. She attended a year and a half at Spalding University in Louisville and later graduated with a B.A. from Northwood University and is currently working on ESL Certificate from Asbury College.

Daniel did kindergarten at Christian Academy of Louisville, skipped first grade, and entered second grade at Ndola Trust School. He attended Blake Elementary School in Louisville for fourth and fifth grades. Daniel entered sixth grade at Trichardt School for Christian Education, did eighth grade at Bruce Middle School in Louisville, grades 9 and 10 at Trichardt, and then graduated from Southern High School in Louisville, KY. My only attempt to home-school Daniel was in Algebra through the University of Nebraska. Daniel graduated from Johnson University and was awarded an M.A. in Ministry and Leadership at St. Catharine College in Bardstown, KY.

Deborah attended Blake Elementary School in Louisville, Kentucky, for kindergarten and first grade. She did grades 2 and 3 at Trichardt School for Christian Education in Mozambique, grade 4 at Blake Elementary, and grades 5 and 6 at Trichardt. Deborah went to T.T. Knight Middle School in Louisville, KY, for seventh grade, home-schooled in Mozambique for the first half of eighth grade, and finished out eighth grade home-schooling while living in Shepherdsville, KY. She did ninth grade and half of tenth at Christian Academy of Louisville, and graduated from high school through correspondence courses from the University of Nebraska at Lincoln. Deborah completed a Certificate of Christian Leadership at Louisville Bible College.

The above summary serves as proof that the education of missionary kids can be both varied and challenging!

Teaching by Example

As a young girl contemplating missionary service and as a young woman entering missionary service, I thought that teaching people about God was all about WORK. Now I know that teaching people about God is NOT about work; it is about LIVING CHRIST among them.

Teaching people about God means living within my own home in a manner that will cause my children to know Him. Praise God that all five of my children have accepted Christ as Lord and Savior! I thank God today that I had a husband that insisted that my priority as a missionary wife and mother was first to teach my children within my home.

A veteran missionary once expounded that the people one ministers among may quickly forget the sermons preached and the lessons taught, but they will never forget how you lived among them. Teaching people about God means living a life in which those with whom you work and come in contact will see Christ in you.

When I think back over 23 years of life in Zambia and Mozambique, I remember countless hours spent in church services, seminars, conferences, and classrooms. Innumerable sermons and teachings were prepared and delivered. But what do the people remember most? They remember the way we lived among them. People from blocks and miles around us in both Zambia and Mozambique recognized us wherever we went. They watched the way we lived – every step we took, every move we made.

Remember Ba Jenipher I told you about in the "Make Disciples" section? Remember what she said: "Bana Miriam, you have taught me many things from the Bible, but I learned the most about living a Christian live by being with you in your home. I saw how you treated your husband and how your raised your children. Now I know how to live as a Christian."

Remember Clodie? I told you about her in the "Make Disciples" section, too. Seven years after we left Zambia, Clodie obtained our address in Mozambique and wrote to say thank you for showing her Jesus.

Daniel and Deborah both had many friends among the Mozambican nationals. When we first arrived in Mozambique, there was a big empty field in front of our house. Daniel, who was 11 at the time, recruited his new friends to make a soccer field. They all came with their tools and hoed and raked and carried off rocks until the field was level and clear enough to play on. They took balls of string and tied their own net and made balls from plastic bags and rubber bands. Every day, droves of boys came from the village to play on that field.

Pedoa, one of the boys who came to play, always brought his baby brother and set him on the ground at the edge of the field. The child would never move from that spot.

One day Daniel, visibly upset, came to me asking if I had a black dress. I said I did and then asked, "Why?"

"It's for Pedoa's mother," Daniel said. "Her baby has died."

Daniel took my black dress, gathered clothes from every member of our family, put them in a big, black garbage bag, got on his bike, and pedaled to Pedoa's house. Pedoa's family has never forgotten Daniel's ministry to them that day. He didn't preach a sermon; he didn't teach a class; he simply showed them that he loved and cared.

In a similar vein, Daniel did the same thing again when he arranged a New Year's Eve party on the soccer field for all the boys in the village. He went through his closet and chose items for each of the boys so that every one of them would have something "new" to wear for the new year. Again, he simply taught the love of Christ through his life. Many of these boys (now young men) are following Jesus and active in the church that meets on the compound where they first experienced this love.

During our last year in Mozambique, Deborah was friends with three Mozambican girls who were our neighbors. Her best friend was Belinia. One day Belinia came to us in much distress to say that her mother, a very young woman, had died. Deborah put on her funeral clothes and put off her American ways to accompany Belinia in mourning the death of her mother. A few months later, Belinia returned to our house – this time to mourn with Deborah the death of her father. Deborah cared and comforted Belinia; Belinia, in turn, followed that example and cared and comforted Deborah.

Example after example comes to mind of those who were touched, not only by what was preached and taught, but also by how we lived. In the years since Cecil's death, there has been an outpouring of letters and messages from Zambia and Mozambique in which people have expressed how their lives were changed just by our presence among them – members of the Zambia national softball team, Frikkie the butcher, friends and casual acquaintances, church leaders and members, neighbors and friends.

Remember Lawrence in the "Make Disciples" section? The man Cecil found in prison? When Lawrence was released from prison, he became a frequent visitor in our home, a companion to my husband, pastor of an English-speaking church, chaplain with Prison Fellowship Zambia, and later a professor at an interdenominational theological college in Ndola.

Upon hearing of Cecil's death, Lawrence wrote this letter to me:
"Dear Mrs. Byrd,

We were grieved to learn of Bro. Cecil's promotion to eternity. We heard how he died defending the cause of Christ and his family. We pray for you, my dear sister, and for the family that you will continue to be strong in the Lord.

As for me, I really thank God for Cecil. Because he cared enough to follow me up when I came out of prison, I am still standing. His stand on what the Scripture says and his doing what the Scripture demands was a powerful example to me. His love to take the Gospel where it has not been heard or where it has least been heard is exactly the same as what I am doing now. The seed he planted in me is growing.

So be assured that his ministry into my life continues to bear fruit. We thank God for letting us know Him."

You were right, Max Ward Randall. They will never forget how you lived among them. Teach by example.

I Am with You Always

Yes, He was! The following excerpts from our lives prove it.

Birth Stories

I still remember how my body shook and trembled when I realized I was in labor with my first child. God was with me then and for four more births as well. There's no way I could leave these birth stories out of this section.

Firstborn Son

Soon after we celebrated our first year of marriage, I became pregnant with our first child. Cecil was a second semester junior at Johnson Bible College, and I was working as the new business clerk for Prudential Insurance Company in Knoxville, Tennessee. On weekends, Cecil was preaching at Bloomington Christian Church in Byrdstown, Tennessee. He began at Bloomington as the youth minister, under the guidance of Mike Sabens, who was preaching at both Bloomington and Byrdstown Christian Church. When Mike became the full-time minister at the town church, Cecil became the minister at Bloomington.

One of the members at Bloomington, Tommy Copeland, was married to Dr. Billy Copeland. When I became pregnant, I began seeing Dr. Copeland in hopes that our baby could be born in Byrdstown. We stayed with people in the church when we drove in from Knoxville on the weekends, but toward the end of my pregnancy we rented a trailer from the Dr. Copeland's wife. We were so excited as we moved into the trailer, planning that I would stay in Byrdstown until the baby was born. On the weekend that I was supposed to stay, however, our best-laid plans changed.

During the church service that day, Cecil called on an elder to pray, and the elder refused. Cecil couldn't believe that an elder wouldn't pray. So, Cecil walked out of the church. He said he wasn't going to preach in a church where elders wouldn't pray. He did not take into consideration that this was a little country church, and the people in it were quite shy. We went back to the trailer and packed up everything that we had just moved down there and transported it all back to Knoxville.

Eventually, there was reconciliation with the Bloomington church. They were not upset that he had walked out; they were upset that he was no longer the minister. They really loved us and had become so much a part of our lives.

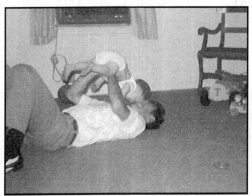

They had given us a wedding shower and, a year and a half later, a baby shower. At both we received handmade quilts from the ladies. We often benefitted from the fruits of their gardens and the craft of their kitchens.

The church contacted Johnson Bible College. Dr. Floyd Clark, the Academic Dean, made a trip to Bloomington with Cecil. Cecil apologized, and the church asked him to come back as minister. By then, however, Cecil was already preaching at Woodlawn Christian Church. Dr. Clark advised, as well, that it might not be best to go back to Bloomington as the minister as there could still be a wound there. Years later, when we were raising support, Bloomington became one of our $100 a month supporters. They partnered with us for years and years. There was a good relationship. We went back for revivals, for vacation Bible schools, and just because the doctor's wife owned Star Point Boat Dock and several cottages on Dale Hallow Lake. Cecil loved

fishing, and Tommy would invite us to stay in the cottages and use the pontoon boats and fishing boats. She gifted us with an acre of land on the land above the lake in preparation for the time that we could build a log cabin and retire. After Cecil died, I sold the land and used the money as part of the down payment on a house in Louisville.

Before the reconciliation happened, however, we had to find a doctor in Knoxville who would take me as a patient in my last month of pregnancy. I was shocked and heartbroken and found it no easy thing to find a doctor. Finally, a couple of weeks before the baby was due, Dr. Jensen had mercy and took me in.

There was no public ban anywhere on smoking in 1971. As we were sitting in the waiting room of Dr. Jensen's office, people were smoking. I was sitting next to a pregnant lady who lit a cigarette. Cecil said to her. "That's harmful to your baby's health and harmful to everyone else in here." That didn't make her too happy. But thankfully, they called me to go back into the doctor's office, and I wasn't witness to what happened after that. That's not the end of the story, however. When I went to deliver my baby, that lady was in labor, too, and ended up being my roommate in my semi-private room! She managed to get herself transferred to another room very quickly.

The baby was due on October 13. Of course, we didn't know if the baby was a boy or a girl. Cecil was really counting on a boy. He had chosen the name – Benjamin ("son of my right hand") Curtis (after his dad and himself). Except for the Bloomington incident, the time leading up to the birth was a very happy time for both of us. I quit work a little before I had to because Cecil so much wanted me to be at home. He had a job on campus painting during the summer and was preaching on weekends, so we had two incomes already. We moved from the one room in the dorm in Bell Hall to a little white cottage right on the French Broad River. I immediately planted red geraniums that someone had given me along the side of the cottage. We were so happy with our first little "house" which consisted of one big room in which our bed folded up into the wall during the day, a tiny bathroom, a tiny kitchen, and a tiny study room in which we eventually put our baby's crib. Our little green dining table that Linda Williams had given us when we moved into Bell Hall was placed in front of the picture window so that we could look at the river at every one of our meals together. Electric heat came through coils in the wall. It was a cozy little place with a red vinyl chair and tan vinyl sofa furnished by the school. My parents gave us a rocking chair (plus the crib) when the baby was born. Then we owned three pieces of furniture – the rocking chair, the crib, and the green table for two. A few months later, Ed Peterson gave us a television that he had dug out of the trash when he was collecting garbage for the city of Knoxville. It had no picture, but it had sound. After Ben was born, I would listen to "Dragnet" while Cecil was in chapel and I was nursing my baby boy each night.

It was a lovely summer. Just before school started in August, we went to Gatlinburg to Christus Gardens and to the Carriage House Restaurant on Chapman Highway. It was so much fun – our last hurrah as a couple, I suppose. Then school started. It was Cecil's senior year. I had quit school at the end of the first semester of my senior year to get married and go to work. At that point, I needed only eight credit hours to graduate. I took Restoration History by correspondence and another course (some kind of theology?) and then had only four hours of senior Bible left, which I was saving to take with Cecil during his senior year. Some people thought I was crazy to quit school with only eight hours of credits left, but I did not doubt that I was going to finish. So when our new baby was two months old, his mommy went back to school. Patty Martin took care of him for four hours each week while I was in class.

October 13 came and went. The baby didn't come. There were four student wives due between October and December that year. The first girl went into labor, and a very sad thing happened. The umbilical cord wrapped around the baby's neck, and the baby died. That was very, very sad. The remaining three of us were unsure of what to do. Should we go to her, still carrying our babies within our bodies? We finally did, but she was very depressed.

I kept waiting, and didn't have a baby. Didn't have a baby. Didn't have a baby. Didn't have a baby. Fifteen days passed. October 28 came, and Cecil had a psychology test the next day. It was evening, and he was studying at the little green table in front of the picture window. I began to feel some contractions, and I said, "I think I might be in labor." He got really excited, and I started trembling. All of a sudden, I was so cold. I was trembling all over and so cold, even though the weather had not turned cold at all. We didn't have a phone, so Cecil had to run up to the top of the hill quite a ways to that very same phone booth in which I had first seen him and fallen in love. But before he ran, he turned on the coil heater in the wall. I stood in front of the heater, trembling. Cecil returned and said that the doctor said to come to the hospital.

We left for the hospital between 9 and 10. The nurse prepped me for delivery. She was not very patient, kind, or understanding, and I was nervous – not really knowing what to expect. What happened next was twelve long hours of labor. Cecil was in the waiting room as it was not common for fathers to be in the labor and delivery rooms in the early '70s.

Around 1:00 p.m. the next day, October 29, a bouncing eight-pound, half ounce, twenty-one inch baby boy was delivered into the world. I wasn't aware of it, however, as I was under anesthesia. The last thing I remember is that they broke my water and took me to the delivery room. The first thing I remember, after hours of labor, was the sound of the nurse's voice (a nice nurse this time) saying, "Mrs. Byrd! Mrs. Byrd! Wake up, Mrs. Byrd. You have a baby boy!" I remember groggily replying, "Is it over?" It had been so my desire to have this baby naturally, but the doctor wouldn't allow it. He had already told me before, "There is no way I'm going to let you deliver without anesthesia." Little did I know that I was blessed to have missed the episiotomy and the forceps while under anesthesia. I felt the effects of both for weeks afterward, however. It was hard to walk, hard to sit, hard to stand.

Finally, the baby was here, and I was so happy to have a baby boy, so that my husband wouldn't be mad at me! The nurses called him, "Bright eyes." He had big blue eyes and was always looking around.

I was in the hospital for four days, doing sitz baths to help with the stitches and making sure all of my body systems were working properly again. The nurses kept reminding me that, if I didn't go to the bathroom, they were going to insert a catheter.

Evelyn, the office manager, and Frieda, another co-worker at the insurance office, came to visit. They gave me a beautiful yellow quilt and pillow for the baby. They said, "What a beautiful baby boy!" and made me promise to bring him to the office to show him off.

Four days after Ben was born, we took him home. It seemed like the whole world had changed in those four days. I had gone to the hospital on a beautiful fall evening. I remember enjoying the beautiful leaves along the river bank on the afternoon before going into labor. When we left the hospital, however, it seemed that every leaf had fallen off the trees. It was gray and cloudy and the wind was cold. I was nervously holding this bundled up baby in my arms. My parents came for a few days and helped out with cooking and cleaning and caring for the baby. So many people from the college came. The staff was so

nice. I was overwhelmed with their love and service. They were all bringing food and presents and praying with us. It was fun, even though I was spending the days and nights in my flannel gowns.

By the end of six weeks, Ben was eating fruit, cereal, vegetables, and meat, drinking sugar water from a bottle, and breastfeeding. We went back to North Carolina and Virginia for Christmas break to show off our baby to everyone. Everybody was thrilled. My parents got him a little rocking horse for Christmas and a bird mobile as well as a little red sleeper with a Santa hat.

Ben loved the bird mobile. He would lie in his crib on his little Mickey Mouse crib sheets and kick his feet. The little plastic birds would flutter all around. There were no sounds, no music, just lots of fluttering colors that kept him quite entertained. This and the blanket game kept him entertained for most of the six months we lived in the little cottage by the French Broad River.

God was with us.

Our Yellow Rose of Texas

After Ben was born, I was eager to have more children – hopefully by the time he celebrated his second birthday. That didn't happen. A couple of months after that, however, I found that I was pregnant with my second child. I was very happy – but also sick with a morning sickness worse than I had experienced with Ben. I ate lots of crackers and drank hot tea, but nothing seemed to help.

On Mother's Day, 1974, we announced to the church in which we were ministering in Campbellsville, KY, that we were expecting our second child. It had been quite a deal to keep Cecil from announcing the news before that! The congregation was very happy to be expecting a new preacher's kid at Woodlawn toward the end of November.

Little did we know at that point that we would not be at Woodlawn when our baby was born. A few weeks later, Al Hamilton came to speak at Woodlawn. Al was beginning a new work called Pioneer Bible Translators. We were very interested in missions and had begun praying that God would raise up workers from within the church at Woodlawn. We did not know that God would use Al to point us in the direction of missions.

Two weeks after Al's visit, we had resigned our ministry, sold our furniture, and packed up a little U-Haul trailer with Ben's crib and toy box and vey few other earthly possessions. We headed to Norman, Oklahoma, where we studied linguistics through the Summer Institute of Linguistics.

We drove into Norman with the tornado sirens blaring. Dust and debris enveloped us on the interstate, making it impossible to see ahead of us. By the grace of God, we managed to pull off to the side of the road until it all stopped whirling. We arrived at the university and settled into one dorm room with a bathroom on the hall. We barely squeezed in the crib and the toy box. The summer passed quickly as we learned phonetics, phonology, grammar, and field methods and ate lots of canned apricots that had been donated to the cafeteria. We consumed all manner of apricots during those three months at Norman with apricots in some recipe at every meal.

For prenatal care during those summer months, I was able to see the school nurse. Lack of health insurance and lack of income prevented me from seeing a doctor. It had not taken long to deplete the funds from the money tree Woodlawn had given us as a farewell gift.

Our best friends in Norman were the Gilstraps and the Franks. They both had children Ben's age, and both were expecting babies in November! Who would have imagined? All of us finished the introductory course at Norman and headed to the International Linguistics Center in Dallas for the fall semester. Much to our surprise, there we met two more couples who were expecting babies at the end of November or beginning of December.

In Dallas, all five of us pregnant women were able to see a doctor who was a "friend" of Wycliffe Bible Translators. What a blessing with only three months left before the birth of the baby! My pregnancy progressed normally, and my blood pressure only became extremely elevated once when Cecil did not return from an errand in time to take me to my appointment on time. He had stopped to help someone having difficulty along the road. By the time I finally got to see the doctor, he made me lie quietly on the table for quite some time until my blood pressure returned to normal.

David and Sharran Pryor joined us in Dallas that fall. They were the second recruits to Pioneer Bible Translators. They bought my prenatal vitamins for the next three months. Toward the end of the pregnancy, we went for an appointment at Methodist Hospital of Dallas to make financial arrangements. After we signed papers for some kind of financial plan, they agreed that I could deliver the baby there and continue to make payments after the birth. By this time, Cecil was serving in an interim ministry at Bella Vista Christian Church in Garland, Texas. This church was a great blessing to us, both financially and spiritually. They became dear friends; and when we left for the mission field, they became faithful financial supporters. Two couples we met at Bella Vista are faithful to support the account I manage through Team Expansion to this very day, even though the church at Bella Vista no longer exists.

The semester at ILC progressed nicely. As a pregnant mother, I was allowed to take only a half load of classes. I took Advanced Grammar and Advanced Phonology. I loved the grammar class and was at the top of it. Phonology was another story. I just couldn't seem to get the hang of it.

By the middle of November, we were ready for some kind of major tests. I was eager to take the grammar exam. I wanted to keep my standing at the head of the class and was afraid that I would forget everything I had learned in the process of giving birth and adjusting to a new baby.

I began to pray that God would allow me to take the grammar test. God answered positively! November 13 came, and I took the test. I was top of the class! For some reason, that meant a lot to me. My professor was very proud of me.

Then I said to God, "OK, I'm ready to have this baby because I do NOT want to take the phonology exam." It wouldn't have been so bad if I had taken the exam and failed it myself, but this professor had paired us with someone else and we had to work on things together. The guy I was paired with was VERY smart, which should have made me very happy. Instead, it made me not want to take the test even more because he would know how very dumb I was.

So I began to pray again. This time I prayed to go into labor, even though the baby was not due for 11 more days. We got through the day (the grammar exam had been first thing that morning). After supper, Cecil said that he was going to go to prayer meeting at this little black church down the road. He loved going to their services.

I said, "Well, don't be gone long because I'm going to have this baby tonight." No sooner had he walked out the door than I started having contractions. I just kept walking, walking – pacing the floor while he was gone. He finally got home around 11 o'clock. When he walked in the door, I said, "I think I'm going to have this baby tonight!" But the contractions weren't close enough together so went to bed. He slept. I tried, but I just couldn't. I got up and paced some more.

Toward five in the morning, the mucus plug passed. Cecil found a place to call the doctor because we didn't have a phone. We were living in a family dorm at ILC – a new facility – with a big room that included desks and a bed with a kitchenette off to the side and a small space for the children to sleep through an open archway off of the big room.

Cecil said, "You know, there's no gas in the car, and we don't have any money either."

We had to wake up people in the dorm. We were just going to borrow money for gas, but the guy we went to said, "No, you don't need to wait and go fill up your car. Just take my car."

This man worked in the donut shop at night and always brought the left-over doughnuts back to the cafeteria in the mornings.

We had to drop Ben at David and Sharran Pryor's apartment off campus. They took Ben, and we raced through Dallas, running red lights. We got to the hospital in time to wait.

The doctor who was on duty was not the doctor I had been seeing. He was the doctor on call. The doctor I had been seeing had gone duck hunting. The doctor on call was ready to go home when we got there.

He said, "We're going to speed up this process. We're going to get this Byrd so I can go home."

He put me on a drip with pitocin. He got his wish. The baby came quickly. God blessed us with a tiny 5 lb. 4 oz. baby girl. The doctor said she was so small because the placenta had not developed properly. We named our tiny girl Miriam Jannette Byrd. I had been reading linguistics articles all that semester, and one article was written by a Bible translator named Jannette. I became attached to that name and thought it fit beautifully with Miriam.

We were in the hospital for three days. Miriam was jaundiced, so the doctors had to keep her under a light in the nursery. We were due to be discharged on Sunday. Cecil preached at Bella Vista that morning, and one of the members invited him for lunch. By then, I was all ready to go, and he was still eating lunch! He eventually came and picked us up and took us home, and there we were – back in the dorm.

So that was November. We finished out that semester at ILC. We drove from Texas to North Carolina and Virginia and showed off our new baby girl to friends and family. After Christmas, we drove back to Texas and began another semester of linguistics training at the center. By May, Cecil had decided that there was no way he wanted to sit at a desk all day and translate the Bible. He'd rather preach. And so began another adventure.

Praise the Lord! God was with us.

First European Child Born at Fiwale Hill

One reason we did not go to Zaire as missionaries was because the missionary who talked to us about going said that we shouldn't have any more children. We wanted more children!

Kathy was the first of our children born in Zambia. The year was 1978, a year and a half after our arrival. I think I was extremely naïve about the whole birthing process. I didn't have any problems with the first two children, unless you call a forceps delivery for the first one a problem. (I had long forgotten about that!) Maybe that should have been a clue to me that all does not always go well in childbirth. The Zambian women seemed to be giving birth easily all the time!

We had been in language school with the Australian Baptist missionaries on their mission station at Fiwale Hill, a 45-minute drive from our home in Ndola. All of the Australian Baptist missionaries lived on this compound where there was also a church and a clinic. The clinic specialized in well-baby and prenatal care. There were also midwives at the clinic who delivered babies. Beth was the pleasant, red-headed, single midwife whom we came to love. Fiwale Hill seemed like the perfect place to have a baby. We approached Beth with the idea. After some thought, she agreed. Up to that point, she had only delivered Zambian babies at the clinic. There were no doctors, no delivery rooms or operating rooms – just a bed and a midwife. Fiwale Hill was not a place to which Europeans had come to deliver their babies. For us, however, there did not seem to be much of an option. We could not afford the private hospitals financed through the copper mines, nor could we leave the country to give birth in a more westernized place. Beth did all of my prenatal care, and was there at Fiwale, waiting and ready when Kathy decided it was time to make her entrance into the world.

Kathy was due on April 13, my mother's birthday, but she chose to bypass that day and wait it out until April 16. It was, of course, the rainy season in Zambia, and the roads were in very bad condition. For some reason, however, Cecil had loaned our truck to a co-worker in the mission and we were left to drive the co-worker's tiny Fiat along the rough, rutted road to Fiwale. Being that I was already three days past the due date, I have never figured out the logic in that.

Early in the morning, I began to feel twangs of labor coming on. We really needed Kay Watts, our co-worker, to keep Ben and Miriam if we were going to go out to Fiwale, so we waited until church services finished at Ndola Baptist Church that morning and met Kay at the door. Once we had transferred the children to her vehicle, Cecil and I drove out to Fiwale Hill.

Kathy came rather quickly compared to the other children. We arrived at Fiwale just about 1:00 p.m, and Kathy was born a little over an hour later. No problems whatsoever. It was hard on Cecil, however. That was the first time he had been with me during labor. Every time I'd have a contraction, he would say, "Oh, Betty, I'm so sorry. I'm so sorry, Betty. I'm so sorry!" Finally, Beth, the midwife said, (in Australian accent) "Cecil? Would you like to go to the house and have a cup of tea?" I think Cecil's apologies were beginning to get on her nerves. Or maybe she saw that it was not helping me. It was too late to be sorry! Cecil went up to Beth's house, and Kathy was born afterward.

After the birth, Beth moved us into the big room with all of the Zambian ladies and their new babies. The room was full because every new mother was accompanied by her own mother, sister, or aunt who would care and cook for her.

Kathy and I spent the night there in the ward. Kathy was in a little wire basket next to my bed. I went to sleep and when I woke up, all the ladies in the ward were standing around the bed staring at us! By 9:00 a.m., we were out of there! I was so glad to go back to my house in Ndola.

For a week after I came home, Kay came every day to cook and care for us. No wonder we named our baby for her!

Kay and God were with us.

Umukulu

January 27, 1982--the day Daniel Wells Byrd came into the world.

It had been a beautiful pregnancy with no problems whatsoever. We eagerly awaited the birth of our fourth child. Everyone was hoping for a boy--Ben, because he had two sisters already; and Miriam and Kathy because it was time for a change. Cecil and I were ready to even out the numbers as far as gender was concerned. We had his name picked out: Daniel (from the Bible) and Wells for my dad.

For months, we had been driving 45 minutes south of Ndola, Zambia, out to Fiwale Hill Mission so that Beth, the Australian mid-wife, could follow the pregnancy. Having had such a good experience delivering Kathy at Fiwale, I was more than confident that Daniel's delivery would also go well.

I cannot now remember when the beginning pangs of labor occurred; but I do remember that somewhere around noon on January 26, Cecil and I headed to Fiwale in whatever pick-up we owned at that time. We had waited for Ben and Miriam to get home from school. Our next door neighbors, the Sagars, then "adopted" Ben, Miriam, and Kathy for what they thought would be a few hours until the baby was born.

Daniel's birth took longer than we expected. After more than a day and still no baby, the decision was made to head to Mpongwe Mission about another hour's drive down a rather rough dirt road to the Swedish Baptist Hospital. Mpongwe housed a much bigger facility than Fiwale, and there was an operating room and a doctor on staff. I had seen Dr. Gunar Holmgren on occasion during his one day a week practice in Ndola.

Dr. Holmgren received us gladly. He felt that I had worn myself out in labor and needed some added energy to continue. He put me on a glucose drip and encouraged me to push some more. Cecil, being adverse to pain, decided not to stay in the delivery room, so he slept in the truck outside the door of the delivery room. Just before midnight on January 27 after 36 hours of labor, a whopping big baby boy entered the world, weighing just an ounce or two under 9 pounds and measuring 22 inches long. Dr. Holmgren stuck his head out the delivery room door and called the dad in to see his new baby boy. Dr. Holmgren held Daniel up in the air and gave thanks to God for this beautiful, healthy baby.

The bad thing about delivering at Mpongwe was that mother and baby were required to stay in the hospital for four days, unlike Fiwale when we could get up and leave almost immediately. Daniel, in his little wire basket, and I were taken to the maternity ward. We were given a room to share with a Zambian woman who had recently given birth. Her baby, however, was not in the room with her because she was born prematurely.

She was very, very, very tiny. The baby was kept in another room, the preemie nursery, swaddled in blankets, laying under a light. There was no incubator. The nurses brought the baby to the mother to feed with a medicine dropper. There was a distinct difference in size in that baby and Daniel. In fact, there was a distinct difference in the size of Daniel and all of the other Zambian babies in the hospital. Hence, the nurses named him Umukulu--the Big One.

Cecil hurried back to Ndola (we were now about an hour and a half from the city) to carry the news of the birth of Daniel. No working phones at Fiwale or anywhere near it. No working phones at Mpongwe or anywhere near it. No working phones anywhere between Fiwale and Mpongwe. Actually, I seriously doubt that the Sagars' phone was working , either. Not many phones in Zambia worked in 1982 with any consistency whatsoever. What were the children and the Sagars thinking by now?

Meanwhile, back at Mpongwe, Daniel and I settled into our routine. Early in the morning, I made my way down to the communal bathroom and toilet for a shower. There was no hot water, but I surely wanted to be clean again, and before everybody else decided to come down. When I got back, the nurses brought tea and porridge to the ward. The Zambian mothers were served tea with lots and lots of sugar and milk from a big pot. Dr. Holmgren had ordered a tray for me with a sugar bowl so that I could add just the amount of sugar a normal American would add to tea. He said the tea that was made for the Zambian ladies would be much too sweet for me. The really funny thing was that the Zambian ladies rushed over to get my sugar bowl to add more sugar to their tea!

Later in the afternoon, Cecil arrived with Ben, Miriam, and Kathy. Everyone was thrilled with our new addition to the family. He was greatly loved by one and all. It was not long until we would sing to him, "Poor little bug on a wall, no one to love him at all. No one to tickle his toes. No one to wash his clothes. Poor little bug on the wall." You might call that Baby Daniel's song, but there was no truth in it--quite the opposite, in fact. He had an adoring family who were all more than happy to tickle his toes and wash his clothes.

This became the routine for the four days Daniel and I spent at Mpongwe: a cold, cold shower every morning, the ladies taking my sugar, Cecil faithfully bringing the children to visit. I was so glad when the happy day came that Daniel and I could pack up and go back to Ndola with them.

When I think back on Daniel's birth, I am assured again that God was with us every step of the way. He did not leave me nor forsake me in a time of great need. It was scary to be in labor so long, with no baby in sight, no doctor nearby, and nothing to do but keep pushing. I will be forever grateful that Dr. Holmgren obeyed God's call to serve in Zambia and that God put him there for me and for Daniel and for so many, many others.

God knows what we need before we can even imagine it. Praise His Name! He was with us.

Last One

After the long labor and four long days at Mpongwe, you might think that I would be put off at the thought of another baby. I was not! Cecil and I

119

both wanted another child. Knowing that I could be approaching my thirty-eighth birthday before that could conceivably happen, I consulted with Dr. Holmgren (who kept office hours in Ndola one afternoon per week) for his opinion concerning the advisability of having another baby considering the experience with Daniel's labor and delivery added to the fact that I would be approaching 38 before the baby would be born. Dr. Holmgren said there was no reason not to proceed with such a plan.

After receiving Dr. Holmgren's assurance on the matter, I did indeed, conceive another child. Beth, the midwife at Fiwale, confirmed the fact and agreed to serve as midwife for prenatal consultations and labor and delivery. After all, I thought, "Oh, it was just a mistake that it took so long to deliver Daniel – maybe because he was so big."

Even Dr. Holmgren had said, "Well, maybe your muscles have relaxed too much from having all four children."

So I got an exercise bike. I rode the bike every day. I thought, "Whoa, this delivery is going to be a breeze. My muscles will be sooooo strong."

The pregnancy went well. At the end, when weight began to creep up, Beth said, "You had better start eating more umunani (meat and vegetable relishes) and less nshima (the cornmeal staple)."

The children were excited about the prospect of a new sibling, too. Ben even asked to come home from Rift Valley for the birth.

One day when we were talking about the baby, eight year-old Kathy warned, "Don't count your chickens before they are hatched, Mom!"

Four year-old Daniel inquired, "Mom, when is that baby gonna come?"

I replied, "In March."

And Daniel would reply every time, "Are the soldiers going to bring him?"

We asked Daniel, "Daniel, do you want a boy or a girl?"

He replied, "No, I want a baby!"

The day came (March 13 – the exact due date!) when I began to feel contractions. The Sagars once again took charge of the older children, and Cecil and I headed to Fiwale in a pick-up truck. Of course, once again, it was the rainy season. All of my children were born in the rainy season. During the rainy season, the roads were just awful – rutted with occasional very big holes--especially the dirt roads like the last 5 km of road to Fiwale. In fact, when Kathy was born in April, it's really a miracle we could pass at all because sometimes the holes and ruts are so big that you have to drive around – and there's no cleared ground to drive around on.

I was feeling huge, big contractions by the time we were riding over those ruts. Every time we hit a rut and there was a contraction, it was like, "Ahhhh!" Soon I said, "I can't do this! I'm going to walk." So I got out of the truck and started walking to the clinic. I thought, "Anyway, this exercise will speed up my labor."

There was Cecil creeping beside me in the truck. Everyone in the villages along the way were watching and asking, "What is going on with these crazy abasungu (Europeans)?!"

Much to my surprise, anyway, by the time I walked the five kilometers, the labor nearly was stopping. Beth took us into the clinic where she kept me for a little while. By nighttime, no progress was really being made, and I was getting tired. So Beth said, "Why don't you come up to the house and have dinner with us?" So we did.

This was quite contrary to my first two experiences in America where the doctors would not let me eat at all – in fact, insisted that everything be cleaned out of me. Now here I was in Zambia, and Beth was trying to make me eat roast beef, potatoes, and vegetables. "You need your energy! Eat," she said.

But I couldn't eat because I was still in pain, even though it appeared that no progress toward delivery was being made.

After dinner Beth said, "Why don't you just lay down in the bedroom here."

So, I lay down. Cecil lay on the floor beside me. All through the night, there were contractions, but not close enough to awaken Beth,

Then, finally, about two in the morning, I got up, thinking I had to use the bathroom because there was a lot of pressure in my lower back. The bathroom was across the hall from Beth's room. I got to the bathroom door, felt a big contraction coming, leaned against the door frame, and said, "Ahhhhhhhhh-hhhhhhhhhhhhhhhh!"

Beth hopped out of bed and said, "That was a birth groan!"

I said, "Oh, I have to use the bathroom."

She said, "No, that was a birth groan. You're about to have a baby. Let's get down to the clinic." (all this in an Australian accent, of course.)

She and Cecil wanted to drive me down in a car, but I couldn't bear the thought of getting in a vehicle (it is much easier to bear a contraction standing up rather than sitting down), so they walked with me over to the clinic.

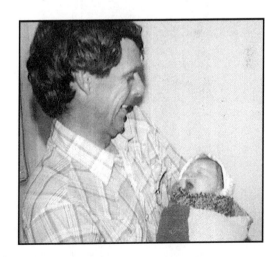

Once we got in the clinic, our precious baby girl was born pretty quickly, almost on the dot of 3:00 a.m. This time, Cecil stayed. It was only a brief period of time that he had to be there. And I'd already said, "If you ever want

to see one of your children born, it has to be this time, because this one is the last one."

Two days later, I wrote the following paragraph in a letter to our forwarding agents:

"Our baby is beautiful and precious. God is so good. Another long labor (38 hours). Stared contractions on the 13th at 1:00 p.m. Deborah was born at 2:55 a.m. on the 15th. Came home 6 hours later. Have felt just great ever since. Cecil stayed with me the whole time – his first time to watch a delivery. He enjoyed it more than he thought he would. Took lots of pictures. Deborah is sleeping long hours. I have rested well since being home."

Truly, God was with us.

Two Weeks in the Country and Already at Gunpoint

Soon after moving in, we went over to Kay's apartment one evening for dinner. As we were returning home, we saw a man walking down the street in front of our house with what looked very much like Cecil's briefcase. (His briefcase was easily identifiable because of the yellow smiley-face sticker on the side). It looked so much like his suitcase that Cecil pulled up beside the man and said, "Hey, that's my briefcase!"

Indeed it was. But the man was not about to give it up. In fact, he pulled out a gun and pointed it at Cecil's head. Then he told me to take the children and run. We ran towards the house.

As we ran, the man repeatedly told Cecil to get out of the truck and lay down in front of it. He did get out, but he refused to lay down. The man got in the driver's seat and drove away with our brand new truck.

When we reached the house, we discovered that we had interrupted a robbery. Our recently newly-organized house was in chaos. Thieves had forcibly entered the back door and proceeded to empty the drawers and cabinets, bundling the desired items into bed sheets which they tied and dropped out of the front windows.

Our neighbor, Mr. Sagar, drove to the police station to pick up a policeman (the phones didn't work and the police had no transportation). I had to giggle when the fat policeman tried to sit in Miriam's high chair from which the tray had been removed.

When the robbery investigation was concluded, it was determined that nothing could be done to recover lost items. After much prayer, however, our truck was discovered a few days later in the place in which it had run out of gas. By God's providence, it had had less than a quarter of a tank in it when it was stolen.

God was with us.

Ba Cecil and Ba Mutyoka Are Dead

The night before our first Thanksgiving in Zambia, Ba Lazlo, an elder at the Lubuto Township church, came to my gate and said, "Your husband has been killed."

He had seen a motorcycle accident and was convinced that Cecil had been killed in the accident.....so convinced that he had walked a very long ways to tell me.

Of course, this was very upsetting news. Not having a working phone, I ran to my next door neighbor's house. He kindly drove Ba Lazalo, Ben, Miriam, and me over to Kay's house. The Davises and Delaneys had already arrived there from Lusaka as we were all planning to gather together for Thanksgiving the next day.

Kay called Howard, the young British pastor at Ndola Baptist Church. He came over, and we were all there, mourning and praying and trying to figure out what to do next. In the midst of this, there was a knock at the door. Kay opened the door, and there was Cecil standing on the doorstep. He had gone home, and we weren't there. The next door neighbor told him what had happened, and he rushed over to 16 Kuomboka Crescent. "No, no, we're not dead. That wasn't Ba Mutyoka's motorcycle," he said.

We had much for which to be thankful that Thanksgiving....Ten weeks in the country and two traumatic events under our belts. Of course, after that, I always had to think when he didn't come home, "OK, is he dead or not dead?"

Because the roads were bad, and we didn't have a four-wheel drive vehicle, he was always getting stuck somewhere. So, I actually planned his funeral and what I would do many times – many, many times. What will happen if he doesn't come back? Was I going to stay in Zambia? In the end, I had already put a lot of thought into what to do if he really should die.

It took a few years, but we finally made an agreement – don't look for him for 48 hours after you first expected that he would be somewhere. Don't send anybody out looking, due to the fact that once he did not turn up to meet somebody, and they thought that something had happened. So they started searching, and all along he was stuck in the mud in a village. So, the 48 hour rule was instituted: "Don't let anybody look for me unless I've been gone for 48 hours after the expected time of arrival."

God was with us, even in the valley of the shadow of death.

Show Me Your Face

One late afternoon, our family was making our way back from Lusaka to Ndola on the main road that ran north and south in the country. Because of robberies and car jackings along this road, we always tried to be back to Ndola by dark. In fact, sometimes, a curfew was enforced, and we had to be back before 6:00 p.m. Cecil would sometimes take chances by himself – often, I would say – but as a family, we usually tried to be home by dark. After the war in Zimbabwe ended, there were unemployed freedom fighters running around everywhere with AK-47s. There were also lots of potholes in the road, which made it almost impossible to travel the speed limit, lest one should hit a huge pothole and destroy the car. Slowing down for a pothole offered the opportunity for robbers to attack as they waited by the road near those potholes.

This time, however, there was a police roadblock up ahead. They often did that – I guess because there was so much unrest in the country that they were trying to check people out. But you never knew if it was a true police checkpoint, or was it a trick? And sometimes it was police, and sometimes it was soldiers, so you never knew what to expect. We were coming home late and there was a roadblock, so what could we do? It must have been more gray dusk, because I could see the guys pretty well. They stopped the truck, and they came towards us with their AK-47s. One's talking to Cecil, one's talking to me. The one who is talking to me keeps saying, "Show me your face! Show me your face!" So I look at him. "Show me your face!" And I said, "I'm showing you my face!" Well, then Cecil says, "Betty! He wants to see your passport!"

I showed him my passport. We were allowed to proceed, and all ended well. God was with us.

Creaking Wing Window

It was very late at night. We were all asleep in our house at 12 Katutwa Road in Ndola, Zambia. All of a sudden, I awoke with a start; and lots of little pitter-pats were going on my in my heart. From the very back of our house, in the very last bedroom where I was sleeping, I heard at the very other end of the house, "Creeeeeeaaaak." I knew immediately that it was the wing window in the dining room, and the only thing between the wing window and the inside of our house was a flimsy little wire screen. That was very frightening. I've never to this day understood: if I was asleep, how did I hear that wing window creak? It was not an extremely loud sound that would carry from the front of the house to back of the house.

Could it be that the Holy Spirit woke me up? I firmly believe that the Holy Spirit woke me up in order to hear the creaking wing window.

When I heard the sound, I nudged my husband and said, "Cecil! Somebody's trying to get into our house!"

Cecil got up, grabbed the trusty baseball bat, and started creeping toward the dining room wing windows. I cautiously followed him. When we got there, we saw our guard, who was really not much of a guard. He was being marched down toward a building at the end of the property that was being used as an office and a storeroom. Two guys were holding him captive Ba Emerson, our guard, captive. We started shouting, "Kabwalala! Kabwalala! Kabwalala!" ("Thief! Thief! Thief!") Praise the Lord, the two men ran. I think they would have been right in our house if the Holy Spirit had not woken me up, and we had not discovered them.

Later, our trusty guard confessed that he had gone around to the other side of the house, where he fell asleep (intentionally). Somehow or other (whether he heard the sound or whether it was just one of his normal checks on that side of the house or whether the Holy Spirit prompted him), he had come around in time to see the men opening the window. They, of course, had seen him as well.

Not long after that, we put metal bars on all of the windows so we didn't have to worry about wing windows anymore.

God was with us that night.

Hep-Hep-Hepatitis

Hepatitis is a disease affecting the liver. In the person who contracts hepatitis, it causes eyes and skin to turn yellow, and urine to turn a bright orange color. Nausea, dizziness, tiredness, and vomiting are other symptoms and effects of the disease.

During the days Kathy and I spent at Musili Training Center, we both came down with hepatitis. It's no wonder. We were eating the food cooked by the women at Musili and using the outside toilets. The toilets, which furiously attracted flies, were not very far from the outside cooking area.

One Sunday morning in early 1983, we had just arrived for the church service at Chisenge Church of Christ. Ben was sitting beside Kathy in the children's section of the church, and I was holding Daniel on my lap in the women's section. Cecil was sitting on the front row of the men's section, soon to be called on to preach. Ben came over to me in the women's section and said, "Mom, you've got to look at Kathy. Her eyes are really yellow."

I looked, and sure enough, her eyes were very yellow. I alerted Cecil, and we left for the doctor. He confirmed with a blood test that Kathy was, indeed, suffering from hepatitis. Poor Kathy. She had just started reception class at Nsansa School. She missed several weeks of the beginning of school that year. She could not attend until her bilirubin count showed that the hepatitis was gone.

Not long afterwards, I, too, came down with the same symptoms and was diagnosed with hepatitis. So, together, Kathy and I avoided fats, rested, kept our eating utensils separate from the rest of the family, barred visitors, had countless blood tests, and eventually recovered from hepatitis. A few years later, Miriam and Deborah contracted hepatitis. By the grace of God, both recovered, using the same regimen that Kathy and I had learned.

God was with us in sickness and in health.

Sleeping with the Lions
By Miriam Byrd Hans

Note from Miriam: "Mom, in my creative writing class for this week, I had to write a 3 page paper about a childhood memory but from another person's perspective. I chose to write about the time we got stuck in the game reserve from your point of view. I couldn't remember everyone's ages, so some of that might be wrong, and I took some liberty in a couple other things. Anyway, I thought you might wanna read it!"

Note from Betty: "Other than ages, Miriam's account is accurate, except for taking the liberty to make me such a heroine and that I was six months pregnant, rather than having a six month old baby! I thought you might wanna read Miriam's version!"

As if she didn't have enough drama in her life, today she found herself stuck in the middle of an African game reserve, sitting in the hot truck whose wheels sank inches deep into a sandy, dried up river bed. It was supposed to be a leisurely day of wild game sightseeing. All five kids were packed into the truck between the front cab and the long bed which was covered by a canopy. Her fearless husband - who said he knew the route to take - was the driver behind the wheel. It really wasn't supposed to be this hard: just drive, look for animals, squeal in delight, and return to the lodge for a delicious, catered dinner.

Not much seemed to ever end up that easy for her, though. A missionary's wife and mother of five children, there was always something going on. Something or someone always needed attention. Worn out, she wondered if there would ever come a day that that she could wake up from her sleep, make her own plans, and watch them unfold without delirious complications throughout the day. Frankly, at that moment, she didn't know which was worse: being surrounded by fierce man-eating animals who lay in hiding close by under the tall elephant grass and thorny bushes, or being back home, surrounded by workers, church members, and street people, who lived in fierce poverty and were pricked with unabated hunger and debilitating diseases.

The sun's heat was agonizing. It was the middle of summer in this country that sat on the equator, and it had mercy on no one. Adding to the misery was the fact that stifling heat and crying babies don't mix well. The sweat dripped down her hungry 6 month old's head, and she could smell the strong scent of urine that had leaked from the cloth diaper onto the baby's clothes and her dress. Outside of the truck, her husband and sixteen year old son were groaning as they attempted to dig the sand out with their hands from around the tires. The kids in the bed of the truck under the canopy had their heads stuck out the windows, their eyes peeled for any movement in the nearby bushes.

No phones, no CB radios, no contact with other human beings anywhere. No one knew they were there. She shuffled her daughter around on her lap and answered the thousand fearful questions her other children shouted from the window. As usual, she was the one who held it all together. No sign of worry, no sign of fear, only reassurance and strategic planning. She ordered the children not to eat the only remaining food items they had left: a few pieces of Rolos caramel candies. The oranges, mangoes and sandwiches they had packed for snacking on while driving through the reserve were already gone. The water had been drunk.

Her husband and eldest son heard the thirsty complaints and began to dig into the sandy river bed. Deeper and deeper and deeper they dug until water soaked their dirty fingertips. Her husband cupped the water in his hands and let it slip into his empty coffee thermos.

"Let it sit a while before you drink it; that way all the sediment will fall to the bottom."

Those instructions sent nightmares of dysentery running through her mind.

"At least Africa knows how to treat these diseases," she justified to herself. She knew they must eventually drink the water. The antibiotics would have to come later – if there was a later.

The digging was not working; the truck would not move no matter how deep they dug, or how much her husband rocked the truck back and forth with the engine revving. Her son broke a small glass window on the rear of the canopy while attempting to push the truck forward while his dad put it in gear and pressed on the gas pedal. The glass was so hot that a blister was forming on his hand from where he had touched it.

"We've tried it all," her husband said. "There's nothing else we can do – I'm going to walk back to the lodge for help." He was determined and the situation was beyond dire. She could not protest. All eyes were on him as he grabbed a big branch from the river bed to use for meager protection and then disappeared down the long, dirt path he had driven down just hours before. Everyone was silent. The baby was sleeping; unaware of the predicament he was in. There was nothing to say.

With hardly enough time to fully contemplate the severity of the moment, she saw movement at the far end of the path. He was returning, his pace quick, his face tight. "There were lion tracks over top of our tire tracks; I'm not going any farther!"

The sun soon lowered onto the horizon, and the temperature dropped drastically as it always does on the equator. She, her husband, and the five children soon shifted from sweating to shivering. Strategizing yet again, she ordered the children to come into the cab of the truck and take cover under the only means they could: a small green tarp that was often left in the bed of the truck in the instance it might come in handy. She asked her husband to turn on the truck and switch the knob from cool to hot as the seven of them crowded onto the narrow seat and onto each other's laps, while some crouched onto the floorboard under the dash and the steering wheel. They chewed the last few pieces of Rolos and drank the brown water as the night took over and sounds of nearby, laughing hyenas seemed to mock their situation.

Between the baby and the three year old who could not hold their bladders for very long, she was soaked in urine in a couple of hours. This only added to their shivering and discomfort. Ultimately, there was nothing she could do. Children cried, children complained, children cried, children complained. The night drug on and on until the sun soon began rising above the plains to begin its torment once again.

In this country, her missionary husband's task was to build churches, preach, train leaders, drive people back and forth to destinations that would have otherwise taken them a full day to walk, and a myriad of other duties. He had always driven a truck, seeing as a car would never be able to sustain the pot holed, tarmac city roads or the bumpy, uneven dirt roads and paths of the villages. Daily, there would be several people riding in the back of his truck, sitting on the wooden benches he had crafted to fit over the hump of the wheel well. This way, he could fit many more people in the back, and they would not all have to sit on the floor of the bed, cringing with every bump he ran over in the road.

When morning came and the sun was threating its torture through the windshield of the truck, it was as though God himself suddenly planted an ingenious idea into her husband's head as he jumped out of the truck and opened the canopy door. He feverishly began to tear apart the wooden benches, acting like a mad man. She looked on, perplexed. He shouted to his eldest son to come and help, explaining his plan of action just outside of her earshot. Before long, they were all standing outside, watching as her husband and son jacked up the truck and planted the wooden boards under the tires. As he lowered the truck back down and got behind the steering wheel, they watched like spectators at a magic show to see if the trick really would work. With a punch to the pedal, he reversed the truck over the boards and out of the river bed that had held them captive. With no regard to the animals they might disturb, they shouted and screamed in fascination and freedom.

Back at the lodge, dinner was long over, and breakfast had already been served and cleaned up. People were milling around the dining room reading the menu for lunch, a cup of hot tea, or a cold bottle of coke in their hands. As if they were now the animals on display, she noticed the stares and gasps of the guests around them as they saw them appear through the dining room doorway. Soaked, filthy, hungry and weary, they drew an inquisitive crowd which no lion, zebra or gazelle had yet drawn in the history of the game reserve's sightseeing. Used to the scrupulous stares that accompany a missionary's wife, and old hat at dragging around five unkempt children in the dust and dirt of Africa, she purposefully disregarded the fact that she smelled like urine, and she proceeded to do what she did best: plan, strategize, and accept the fact that it may be never that she could wake up from her sleep, make her own plans, and watch them unfold without delirious complications throughout the day.

Note from Betty: You told the story well, Miriam! God delivered us from the mouths of lions, from hunger, and from thirst. He was with us through all the watches of the night.

Meningitis

At two months of age, Deborah contracted meningococcal meningitis. It took over a week for doctors to understand that she had this disease. By that time, she was nearly dead. Dr. Piet Reijer, a Dutch doctor working at a Catholic mission hospital in the bush outside of Luanshya, successfully treated her. After twelve days in the hospital and many prayers offered on her behalf, Deborah was released. Because she had many convulsions during this illness, we were advised to take her for a CT scan in South Africa. The scan showed that the ventricles of her brain were swollen to twice the normal size. She was admitted to the hospital in Pretoria, and a VP shunt was inserted in her brain to relieve the pressure of accumulating fluid. She has since had ten shunt revisions but is happily married and living a normal life. God is good! He is the Great Physician and never left us or forsook us.

A Hole in the Head

One December morning in 1986, I retrieved our financial books from the auditor in Luanshya, Zambia, a 30-minute drive from our home in Ndola. Upon arriving home, I reviewed the auditor's report and realized that all he had done was copy the previous year's report. So, I loaded the children (except for Ben who had ridden his bicycle to his friend's house) in the truck and began the return journey to the auditor's office in Luanshya. As we were driving, I noticed that there weren't many people on the road.

"Could it be because it's lunch time?" I asked myself

As I continued driving, I saw that up ahead lots of people gathered in the road. "Must be a bus broken down," I thought aloud. There was nothing unusual in seeing a bus broken down on the roads in Zambia, so I kept driving.

Suddenly, through the air, a huge rock came hurtling toward me, and I thought, "That rock's going to crash through the windscreen and hit me in the face!"

So, I ducked my head, and the rock did hit me in the head instead.

It must have cracked my skull because blood began streaming from the top of my head down my face. I was clenching the steering wheel and the world around me was turning black!

Deborah was in the car seat beside me, and Miriam was on the other side of her, shouting, "Mom! Mom! Are you all right?"

I replied, "Yeah, I'm all right. I just can't see anything. Everything's black."

And Miriam said, "Well, why are you still driving then?"

Evidently, this brief exchange of words drew me back to reality and consciousness. I slammed my foot on the brake, and the truck came to a stop. If Miriam had not been calling me, I think I would have completely lost consciousness.

Some might say that it was unfortunate that the truck seemed to have come to a stop only yards above the crowd from which the rock had been hurled. Even as the truck came to a stop, I knew God had to have been with me to keep the car on the road and keep us from crashing during that brief time I was unable to see.

Part of the crowd, which evidently was throwing rocks at any moving vehicle, ran swiftly toward the truck, incensed (I learned almost immediately) by the government's removal of subsidy on Zambia's staple food, maize meal.

"Take us to the president! Take us to the president!" the crowd demanded.

"What are you talking about? I'm not taking you anywhere. Look at what you did to me. Look what you've done to my children," I replied angrily (too angry to be frightened initially).

Kathy and Daniel were crying in the back of the truck. The crowd had thrown smaller stones at them through the canopy windows.

"No!" the crowd spokesman responded. " You go tell the president to lower the price of mealie meal." (Mealies are cobs of corn or maize.)

I don't know why they thought I had some pull with the president, but, still angry, I said, "You're crazy. No! Look what you've done to us!"

"Well, then, take us to the president so we can tell him," the spokesman rebutted.

"I'm not taking you anywhere. That's my final answer," I again replied as I began blowing my horn in hopes of attracting attention on the other side of the dual highway where I could now see vehicles were beginning to pass.

One of the passing vehicles was a police Land Rover.

"Help me! Help me! Help me!" I shouted, hanging my head out the window and waving frantically.

And then there was a whole line of police vehicle, all loaded (I learned later) with goods that they had looted from the shops. While crowds hurled rocks at passing vehicles on the highways, other crowds were rioting in the city, breaking into shops, and looting goods.

Finally, a policeman stopped, and I cried, "I want to go home!"

And he said, "Well, go. Turn back and go ."

And I said, "I don't' want to go through that mob of people again."

Finally he agreed, "OK, I'll follow you."

And I said, "I don't want you to follow me! I want you to go first, and I'll follow you."

So finally, he did that, after we agreed on the fact that I did not want him to lead me through the wooded forestry plantation. I felt that could be much more dangerous in many ways than traveling through angry crowds on the main road.

Once we entered the Ndola city limits, I drove straight to the clinic and got my head stitched up and bandaged in a turban-like fashion.

Looking back at all that happened that day, I am amazed to think at how assertive I became and can only attribute that assertiveness to the courage God gave me as He was with me.

And I exerted the same assertiveness when I finally got to speak with the auditor. He fixed that year's report and never audited our books again.

God delivered us from an angry mob. He was with us.

Malaria

Even though all of us religiously took anti-malarial medicine weekly (every Sunday morning), Cecil frequently got malaria because he was always working in the bush. Being in the bush day in and day out made him much more susceptible to being bitten by malaria-carrying mosquitos. He had bad cases of malaria several times. I think the worst time was when he'd gone to Botswana and Zimbabwe for a tournament with the Zambia national baseball team. He became so sick that he couldn't continue traveling with the team. He began hitchhiking back to Zambia.

Late in the day of December 10, 1986, the same day of the riots in the story above, Cecil arrived at our gate in Zambia. The front windscreen of our truck was smashed, I had a turban-like bandage around my head, and Cecil walked right past both the truck and me without noticing any damages. He was so sick that he could barely walk. He just went straight into the house, laid down on the bed, and didn't get out of the bed for 12 days after that. He did not want to eat, and anything he did eat, he threw up immediately.

After that bout of malaria, the doctor said, "If you ever have malaria like this again, you will need to leave the country permanently, because malaria is damaging your liver too much."

We lived in Zambia for five more years after that and another seven years in Mozambique without another severe case of malaria. God was with us. He is good.

God secured Cecil's health. He was with us.

A Night at Trichardt

Trichardt was the school in Mozambique in which I taught and which three of the children – Kathy, Daniel, and Deborah – attended.

It was two days before Thanksgiving, 1993, and Daniel, Kathy, Deborah and I left with Bonna Ray, our co-worker, to drive the 16 kilometers from the Boa Nova compound in to school at Trichardt. When we reached the end of the dirt road, which took us from the compound in Machava to the main road to Maputo where Trichardt was located, we looked to the left and saw a lot of smoke in the distance. We thought perhaps one of the diesel buses was having some kind of problem. From where we sat on the dirt road, it seemed like there could be a road block ahead. We thought we might not get past the roadblock in order to make it to school on time, so we decided to turn right and take an alternate route into town.

As we approached town, however, we observed that things didn't seem to be quite normal. There were not very many cars on the street. It was just not a normal Tuesday morning kind of day, as far as traffic was concerned. When we got to the school, we unloaded. A few other people had arrived, but we soon learned that there had been riots in town – all over town. The smoke we had seen from the end of the Machava dirt road was a by-product of the riots in which people were burning cars. They were upset because the government had raised the price of public transport by chappa. A chappa ride came in many forms. A chappa could be a little pickup truck in which the driver would pile tons and tons of people. The people would be standing, bumping along in the back of the truck. A chappa could also be a big truck with rails, similar to a farm truck in the U.S., where massive amounts of people could climb in and squash together, along with their luggage, chickens, and bicycles. A chappa could also be a bigger, diesel powered bus with a rack on top for luggage, chickens, and bicycles. This price raise was just as serious as removal of subsidy from the staple food product in Zambia had been.

The people who lived in town already knew about the riots, so they didn't bring their kids to school. It was rumored that the riots were increasing in violence, so those of us who were already there and would have to go out of the city again were encouraged to shelter in place. There was no safe way to go home. That left Daniel, Kathy, Deborah, Bonna, the director of the school, his wife, another teacher, and me to spend the day and the night at school. There was no food and no beds or sleeping bags. It was extremely hot, and the mosquitoes were TERRIBLE – eating us alive. For the sake of protection, we were all crammed into the little office space in the school as it was the only room with a working lock.

Later we learned later that Cecil and Bonna's husband, Jon, learned about the riots in town and attempted to come into town to rescue us. They were forced by mobs of people on the roads and army tanks overrunning the markets to return to the compound.

But, at dawn's early light, Bonna had a plan.

She said, "Before the city wakes up again, we're going to get in the vehicle, and we're going to race back to Machava!"

I'm not usually a risk-taker, but we were miserable enough to agree.

We jumped in the truck and raced back to Machava without coming into contact with any rioters or revolutionaries. And then, finally, there we were, safely back in Machava on the Wednesday before Thanksgiving with an incredibly lot for which to be thankful.

Yes. God was with us!

Mice in the House

God was with us in some mighty big situations, and He was also with us in what some might consider trivial. Was it important that God was with us when there were mice in the house? Yes, indeed, because I hate mice and go into a panic at the sight of even one. I could have had a heart attack as much as I screamed over mice.

There seemed to be nothing we could do about mice because we had inherited seven hectares of land on which the mice had lived from time immortal. When we started clearing land on which to build a compound, the mice were desperate to find a place to live. When the houses were built and winter arrived, the mice were not happy. They did not like staying outside in those cold fields when we had built houses on their land, so they entered our cold, concrete brick homes. If they couldn't come in by the doors, they would climb up the rough stucco walls to the roof. We could hear them at night racing along the roof. Then they discovered the openings between the roof and the walls, purposely constructed that way to allow airflow during the hot summer days. The mice learned that they could access these openings and then crawl down the inside walls of our houses. They mice especially loved Daniel's room because he often brought his peanut butter and jelly into his room. The mice could smell it and would crawl down his wall to find it. Once he was lounging on his bed when a mouse crawled down the wall and landed on his chest. Better him than me!

My first experience with mice in Mozambique occurred shortly after we arrived. We were staying in a house where a box of blankets was stored. We didn't know it at the time, but the mice loved that box of blankets. They discovered it and made a nest in the bottom of the box. When the owners moved in and unpacked their box of blankets, they found a whole family of mice living there. I don't know what the outcome was for that family of mice because I fled the scene immediately. Disgusting!

Cecil and Daniel were always on a quest to rid our house of mice. They would take brooms and mops and shoes or whatever was handy, move the furniture, and corner the mice. They then took the shoes and smashed the mice, and I would

133

scream the whole time, afraid that the mice were going to come after me. They did the same thing with a huge spider. This spider looked like a tarantula, but I was told it was only a wood spider. One day, I opened our wooden door, and there was huge, huge wood spider on it. The spider crawled onto the floor, and the chase began. Daniel hit this spider with his shoe right in the middle of his round, squishy body. Whatever is inside of a wood spider splattered everywhere. And I mean everywhere! In my book, wood spiders are just as disgusting as mice.

The most frightening experience with mice occurred in the living room of our home in Mozambique. In the living room was a bookcase on the bottom shelf of which I stored cloth from which the women could make quilts. One day, I crawled down on my hands and knees to get some material for somebody. When I stuck my hand in the bookcase, out came mice! Being as I was already on my hands and knees, I very rapidly started crawling away. I didn't think to stand upright. I just kept crawling and screaming at the top of my lungs.

Cecil and the children happened to be in the room and were shouting, "What's the matter? What's the matter?" And I was just screaming. I couldn't say anything – just scream. When I finally wore myself out screaming, I asked, "Why didn't somebody help me?"

Cecil answered, "Oh, I thought you had touched the transformer and were being electrocuted. I thought if I touched you, I would be electrocuted, too."

I said, "Oh, well, thank you very much."

But even if I had no other help from anybody else, I always knew God was with me anyhow.

Preparation for the End

15 Months in Kentucky

In April of 1998, we got a call from more than one of our older children, who said, "Mom and Dad, you probably need to come home. Kathy's not doing very well."

They explained the situation. Kathy was both stressed and depressed. They described quite a serious situation. We made arrangements with our teammates to come home for furlough early. So, in April we left. We came back to Kentucky. We didn't have a place to live because somebody was living in the mission house. We stayed at my sister's house until we found a nice looking house on Charleswood Avenue to rent.

Ben and Katie were getting ready to be married. We were there for their wedding in June. And a year later, we were still home for Miriam and Charlie's wedding. We got to spend a lot of time with Kathy and helped her get an apartment of her own. That whole year we had a lot of good contact with all of the children. When I look back now on those unexpected fifteen months in the U.S., I really do believe that God gave us that specific period of time to spend all together as a family before Cecil's impending entrance into eternity. For the older children, Ben, Miriam, and Kathy, those final fifteen months were unlike any other months that they had spent with their dad. Those months were God's gracious gift to us as a family, especially to the older children, as part of the preparations for the end.

Back to Zambezi

We came back to Mozambique in July 1999, and in October 1999, Cecil and Daniel went back to Zambezi. When we had left Zambia, Cecil had said to Daniel, "We will come back."

Fishing was Cecil and Daniel's favorite thing to do as father and son. In October of 1999, they packed up the truck and drove back to Zambia. They spent two weeks fishing on their favorite river, the Zambezi. This trip, I believe, was God's precious gift to Daniel in preparation for his dad's impending departure from this earth. Such a good gift!

30th Wedding Anniversary

Another gift from God: December 19, 1999, our 30th wedding anniversary.

We'd always said we would go to Cape Town for our 25th wedding anniversary, but we didn't. We went, instead, to a little waterfall near God's Window and not far from Nelspruit, South Africa.

So I thought for our 30th wedding anniversary, we might go to Cape Town, but we didn't.

Cecil had made a plan with a man in Nelspruit near the game park in South Africa. The man said we could use his little cabin on the lake. We understood it would just be our family. Of course, Daniel and Deborah were going with us. I didn't like the idea of leaving them on the Mozambique side of the border.

On the Friday before our Sunday anniversary, we stopped at the man's house to pick up the keys. The man said, "Oh, we've decided we'll go with you."

Well, I was not happy! We hardly knew these people, and I did not want to spend my 30th wedding anniversary with them. I just looked straight ahead, because I knew that if I looked at Cecil, I was either going to be really mad or I was going to cry. So I kept looking straight ahead.

Cecil, very wisely – the most wise thing he did in our whole marriage – said to that man, "You know, because this is our 30th wedding anniversary, we would like to celebrate alone as a family. So if you all have plans to go up to the lake, we'll just check in at the game park."

I'm certain that those words saved our marriage that day

We drove back into town and checked around with people for recommendation about where to stay. They told us about a very nice little guest house run by German people. It was outside of the game park and very beautiful. It had lovely gardens and sizeable little bungalows with thatched roofs. Meals were served meals in a common place. It was all very European and very nice. Daniel and Deborah slept in the upstairs loft, and we had the downstairs to ourselves. We were in easy access of the game park. In my opinion, it was much nicer than going to a fishing cabin and fishing!

On the road to the place we stayed, we passed a farm that had roses growing everywhere along the fences. On Sunday, the day of our anniversary, two guys on a motorcycle drove up to our bungalow and delivered 30 roses. Cecil had returned to the farm alone to arrange this special delivery with these men. When the roses arrived, Cecil gave me a gold Africa pendant to commemorate our life together in Africa. I wear that pendant around my neck daily to this day. What a very special 30th wedding anniversary, more special than any of the 29 that preceded it. I believe it was orchestrated by God as a gift I will never forget, one month and one day before Cecil left this earth.

A Day at the Beach

We lived in the city of Maputo, Mozambique. If you look at the map, it looks like Maputo is right on the Indian Ocean, but it's really not because the bay around the city separates it from the ocean. The bay is very dirty and smells like fish. Some people would go there to swim, but we always held out for the ocean. To get to the ocean, it was necessary to catch a ferry that took you across the bay to a beautiful, beautiful beach.

Cecil did not like to go to the ocean. He wasn't fond of beaches and he didn't like swimming. He preferred rivers for fishing and basketball for sports. So in our seven years in Mozambique, we may have gone to the beach seven times, mostly on those occasions when there were visitors from America.

Not only did Cecil not like the beach, but he also didn't like the ferry that took you to the beach. It was kind of a rickety old ferry, and, if truth be known, probably dangerous to be riding. There was always a gap between the ferry and the land, making it difficult to embark on the ferry. There was a fear of injuring your vehicle just getting on the ferry. There seemed to be an art to it. Parking on the ferry was also a nightmare. Cars were all smashed up against each other. The attendant didn't let you park where you wanted to park; you had to park where he told you to park. At this time, we had a new truck, and Cecil didn't want his truck messed up. So, we rarely got to go to the beach and never at Cecil's suggestion.

But here we were, in January. It was the day before the new school year started, and Cecil said to Deborah, "Deborah, you can invite some of your friends and I'll take you to the beach today. It will be your last hurrah before school starts."

So Deborah invited her friends, and Cecil took them to the beach. He spent the whole day there with them. Deborah will always remember that day at the beach, two days before her dad was killed. She remembers how he didn't like to go to the beach, yet he had offered to take her without her even asking. I see that as a special gift from God in preparation for the end that was so near.

God was more than with us. He gave us gifts of precious time and memories.

January 20, 2000

Very early on the morning of January 20, 2000, Daniel and Cecil drove our truck four hours down the road to Nelspruit, South Africa to repair leaks in the canopy. The plan was to use the vehicles, beginning the next day, for sleeping during a four-day seminar in the bush of Mozambique.

Deborah and I invited Tim, an intern living on the compound, for supper and a game of Monopoly. Around 8:00 p.m., while we were about to wrap up our game, we heard the truck pull up beside the house, and Daniel came inside. I asked, "Where's your dad?"

Daniel replied, "He's finishing a tape he was listening to in the truck. He'll be in soon."

Daniel headed toward his room and then out to visit with his friends staying in the Hawkes' house on the compound; Deborah, Tim, and I continued with our game.

"Whew! I'm so tired!" Cecil commented as he came through the front door a few minutes later.

"Want some supper?" the good wife in me dutifully asked.

"No. I'm so tired. I just want to drink this Coke and go to bed," he said as he grabbed a bottle from the crate (we purchased Cokes by the crate from the Coca Cola factory down the road) sitting next to the freezer in the dining room. "Have to be on the road for the seminar early in the morning."

"OK. Goodnight!" I sang out cheerfully, being as I was winning at Monopoly.

A little while later, I was proclaimed the victor, and Tim returned to the duplex below us. The front of Tim's duplex faced the back of ours, just as the front of our duplex faced the back of the duplex where the Brooks family lived. Deborah and I cleaned up the game, and she went to her bedroom to enjoy music via her headphones. As I finished tidying up the dining room where we had been playing, Daniel came back in, locked the front door, and went to his room.

A few minutes later, as I put on my eleven year-old, cool, threadbare, ripped-down-the-side cotton nightgown (January was the hottest month of the year in Mozambique) and sat on the side of the bed before lying down, I heard gunshots in the distance.

Daniel came into the bedroom from his own room across the hall, imploring, "Mom! Mom! Did you hear those gunshots?"

Unalarmed, since we frequently heard gunshots in the area, I replied, "Yeah."

"Those shots were on the compound. We've got to wake up Dad!" Daniel shouted.

By then, we could hear pounding on the door of the house below us where Tim was living. Cecil woke up, dazed from a deep sleep. Cecil and Daniel began blowing whistles and shouting in an attempt to get the attention of the guard at the front of the compound. Little did we know that the shots Daniel and I had heard earlier went straight into the stomach of the unarmed guard. From our bedroom window, we could see Tim run through the front door of his duplex, jump over the fence that divided our property from his property, and continue running by the side of the house, where we could no longer see him. He later told us that he jumped the side fence as well and climbed a cashew tree in the Hulseys' front yard.

Not far on Tim's heels out the front door of that duplex came four men armed with AK-47s.

I began shouting, "We gotta get Deborah! We gotta get Deborah!"

Deborah was on the other side our house, a duplex which had been opened up to serve as one big family dwelling for a larger family.

Cecil left our bedroom with the only weapon we had, a baseball bat. Daniel paced in front of the bedroom window, praying, "Lord, protect my family! Please protect my family!"

I visibly trembled, silently praying. No words would come out of my mouth.

Suddenly, the thieves were pounding on our back door. About the time Cecil got to where the duplex divided, the thieves were in our house.

Deborah, even though she had earphones on, listening to music, heard the gunshots, too. Also hearing someone yelling, she took off the headphones and carefully peeked out her window to see what was going on. She could see nothing. Then she heard the whistle being blown in our house. She remembered her dad had telling her never to blow the whistle unless there was trouble, so the sound of the whistle alerted her to the fact that something was up. She came out of her bedroom and spoke into the dark, "What's going on?" She heard her dad reply, "Deborah, get down!" Again she asked, "What's going on?" and again she heard in reply, "Deborah, get down!" She heard a lot of yelling outside, so she crawled underneath the coffee table and lay there listening to all the commotion. She saw her dad run behind the living room couch toward the dining room door to open it and then saw a man kneel behind the couch with an AK-47 and aim at her dad. To this very day, she still remembers the smoke and the smell that came from that gun. The man then ran toward her dad, and Deborah ran to the bedroom to join Daniel and me.

Evidently, the thief then chased Cecil back toward the bathroom outside of Deborah's bedroom. I heard another shot and Cecil's deep groan. That was the last I heard from that side of the house. I was pretty sure that he was dead because I never heard another sound from him and he didn't come back to rescue us.

Having taken care of the threat which Cecil must have posed to them, the four thieves returned to our bedroom with their AK-47s in hand.

I tried to hold the door shut so the men could not enter; but, of course, that was futile.

Daniel said, "No, Mom, you've got to let them in. They might try to shoot through the door."

So I quit trying to hold the door shut. They opened the door, and I was behind it. One of them grabbed my arm and threw me on the bed, and I thought, "Oh, please, Jesus, help me!"

Immediately, they began demanding money. We gave them all we had.

They said, "No, no, there has to be more. There has to be more."

They continued waving their AK-47s around and threw my jewelry box at Deborah. We emptied everything out of it, and they threw that at her, too. They kept demanding more money.

Daniel served as the communicator, speaking to them in three different languages – Portuguese, English, and Afrikaans.

Finally, Daniel said, "Just take the truck. Here are the keys. We don't have any more money. Take whatever you want out of the house. That's all we have."

The thieves replied, "No! We want money!"

Again, Daniel said, "We don't have any money."

Perhaps they were at last convinced.

They said to Daniel, "You come with us and show us the way to get off of this compound."

I suppose they realized that people were gathering at the front of the compound where the guard was shot. They took Daniel outside. I could hear them underneath our bedroom window, still demanding more money.

Eventually, they relented and said, "OK, just show us a way to get off the compound."

Daniel took led them to the back hedge where there was a hole in the bushes through which they could crawl.

They turned around and said to Daniel, "OK, you can go now. Just don't call the police."

Unbelievable! Does that make any sense at all in the whole scheme of things?

As Daniel led the thieves to the back of the compound, I crawled from the bedroom to our office across the hall. The phone was in the bedroom, and I attempted to phone for help from someone on the compound. Because it was the long break between school terms, few people were there. Susan Brooks was in the house above us, along with her children and a friend and her children who were staying with Susan while Martin and the friend's husband were at a conference in South Africa. On the other side of the little path beside our house, parallel to the duplex in which Tim was staying, were Manuel d'Oliveira and his wife, Pam. A couple of village boys were staying in Mike Hawkes' house while Mike and his family were in the U.S.

I called Manuel, and I said, "Manuel, can you come and help us? Cecil is dead."

"Are you sure he's dead?" Manuel asked.

"I'm sure he's dead." I replied.

"I'm trying to call the police," Manuel replied.

Unbeknownst to me, Susan, having heard the shots and realizing something bad was happening, was calling friends from other missions.

While I was calling Manuel, Deborah found her dad's body. She was hysterical. While I was trying to comfort her, Daniel came back in the house. I really never expected to see him. I thought he was gone for good, too. He saw Deborah crying, and he was crying, and he said, "Mom, Mom, why did they have to kill my dad?"

By the grace of God, I was calm. Through the work of the Holy Spirit, these words came out of my mouth: "I don't know, Daniel, but I do know that in all things, God works together for good for those who love Him and are called according to His holy purposes."

About that time that Mark Harper, one of the friends Susan called, arrived at our house and took us, and then everyone from the Brooks' house and the Hawkes' house, across the path to Manuel's house where we all gathered to work out a plan. In the meantime, men with whom I worked at Trichardt School arrived and took the guard to the hospital, from which he was released days later in good condition. People from Christian Academy of Mozambique, where Susan worked, came with a van. Eventually, all on the compound were distributed to safe homes for the next few days.

Daniel, Deborah, and I were given a ride to Mark's house, several kilometers away, and there we spent the next four days before returning to the U.S. They were already housing in their not-so-big house twenty-one Youth for Christ workers who were visiting from South Africa. Leslie gave the Daniel and Deborah an herbal drink that would make them sleep. I refused to drink it because there was too much to think about. Stress must have activated my bladder because every fifteen minutes I was stepping over Daniel to go to the bathroom.

At that point, I hadn't called any of the children in the U.S. I suppose I was in shock, and I could not bear to think of having to call the children and tell them that their father had died.

Some have asked me, "Where was God on the night of January 20, 2000?"

My answer is that He was there. He never once left us on that night, or since, for that matter.

Where?
by Miriam Byrd Hans

They say you are omnipresent, ever-seeing and all-knowing
So I was wondering where you were and if you knew how I was coping.
Where were you when my tears fell down like rain;
When I couldn't find a refuge from the grief and from the pain.
Where were you when the nightmares raging in my head
Were too much to handle and they woke me from my bed?
Where were you when thoughts of his death pierced my mind like a sword
And the anger and resentment strangled my heart like a cord?
They say you're a loving Savior; a caring, comforting Lord.
I finally heard your voice and what you were trying to say;
You were trying to show me that you had been there that day.
You were trying to tell me that you hurt – perhaps even more -
When my father met his killers just inside the door.
Yes, you knew what would happen and it hurt you very bad;
But you knew that in time I wouldn't be so sad.
You reminded me that your angels escorted him all the way
And when he reached the heavens, he gazed upon your face.
You were there during my nightmares; you lulled me back to sleep.
You traded my anger and resentment for a supernatural peace.
My head is no longer tormented with the way in which he died;
And my tears are not so many - because of your hand, they dried.
My questions have been answered and now my story is told -
Of an omnipresent Savior, unchanged from days of old.

Images
January 20, 2000, by Betty Byrd

Gunshots in the distance...
Close...
At the thorn bush entrance to the compound...

Before I realize what's happening,
There is kicking and pounding
On the door of the house below...
Near.

Wake up, Cecil, wake up!
Blow the whistle, call the guard.

But the guard cannot come.
He is lying bleeding on the ground.
Four bullets in his abdomen

It's happening quickly.
They are at our door.
Kicking, pounding, entering...

Where is Deborah?
We have to get her from the other side of the house.
She is too young, too vulnerable, to face these men alone.

Cecil leaves the room to get Deborah.
Daniel is pacing, praying, "Lord, protect my family, protect my family.
In the Name of Jesus, protect my family."

Deborah's here now.
Running, ducking, crawling, hiding...
She made it to the bedroom, to us, to me and Daniel.
One last glimpse of her dad on the way.
Bullets whizzing...
Missing her, wounding him in the arm.

Others are with us as well.
Frantic faces, shouting at us, gesticulating...
"Where's the money? Where's the money?"

Gunshots from the other side of the wall.

A groan. Silence.
My husband is dead. I know it as surely as I know that I am still alive.

A man with an assault rifle enters the room.
Demanding faces are still crying for money.
The rifle is roaming, aiming, roaming, aiming.

I resist.
They have taken my husband.
Why should I give them money as well.

Portuguese, Afrikaans, English…
All the languages are repeating the words,
"Where's the money? Where's the money?"

Who are we that they must speak to us in three white languages?
They do not know us as missionaries.
They know us only as white.
White means money.

"Where's the money? Where's the money?"
Rifles roaming, aiming, roaming, aiming.

Daniel jolts me back to reality.
"Give them the money, Mom. Just give them the money."

They have taken all that is important already.
Take the money. Take all of the money.

"Where's the rest? Where's the rest?"

"There is no more. There is no more."
White isn't as rich as it appears.

"Then come with us, boy."

They take Daniel outside.
"Where's the rest? Where's the rest?"
There is no more.

"Then show us a way to leave."
Flanked by four men and an AK-47, Daniel stumbles to the back hedge.
As the men crowd through the thorn hedge, they turn to say,
"If you call the police, we will come back and kill you."

Daniel re-enters the house.
Deborah is searching the rooms for her dad.
She discovers what I already knew.

We check the doors. We cry. We wait.
Alone in the dark.
Afraid to move.

There were gunshots in the distance.
This time they came too close.

Greed
by Miriam Byrd Hans

For the love of money, some men will kill -
For them it will be just another cheap thrill.
They don't care that this man was priceless to us -
They are only driven by insatiable greed and lust.
What they looted that night, they would split four ways;
So they shot him dead and continued their rampage.
The fear of a mother, the pleas of her son:
"We have no more money, please put down your guns!"
A daughter, so scared, she hides in the corner;
She fears she might be next in their line of order.
The killers weren't satisfied and demanded for more
While standing with guns cocked and ready at the bedroom door.
With fear in the room, but courage in his heart,
The son begged them, "Please, take anything you want."
They accepted the invitation and grabbed him by the arm -
Guns held on his back and his head, though he showed no alarm.
"Show us the way out" they yelled. How selfish can men be?
They wanted help after killing his father and terrorizing his family.
He knew his only hope for his life was to concede
So he showed them a way out through the bushes and the trees.

It was over; they were gone; so he began to run.

He didn't realize that the nightmare of grief had only just begun.

The cries of anguish and heartache, he could hear from outside -

Inside, his sister, holding his father, on the floor where he died

The anger, the hurt, the resentment, they would come;

Who would have believed this could ever have been done?

A wife with no husband, and the children, no father;

There will only be a grave with pretty flowers to water.

For so little money they murdered this man

Because of greed in their heart and a gun in their hand.

Even until the End of the World

Life after Death

By the next morning, it was apparent that news was beginning to leak out across the internet.

I thought, "Oh, we can't have this because my own children don't know that their father has died, so please stop sending emails, everybody!"

Mark Harper called our forwarding agent, Ron Flora, and told him the news. Then Ron went to Ben, my oldest son and told him in person. Ben went to Kathy and told her in person. Miriam was in Oklahoma where her husband was in flight school at that time, so Ben called her husband, Charlie, and Charlie told Miriam. Later in the day, I talked to all of three of them on the phone. It was so amazing, because they were concerned for me, and I was concerned for them. I was so worried about how they were doing, and they were so worried about how Daniel, Deborah, and I were doing.

Mark Harper continued to run before us and help in so many ways. Our South African friends had brought the police to the compound after dropping the guard at the hospital. The next day, Friday, the police returned and marked off the house as a crime scene with yellow tape. Mark went back for us that day and retrieved some clothes and personal articles. He also placed a basket of flowers in the spot where Cecil died from the gunshot wound to his chest. People from the U.S. Embassy visited us on Friday. They were all dressed up in white shirts, black ties, suits, and shiny black shoes. They were very kind. Daniel had just met the consular officer the previous weekend when he attended a cookout with one of the embassy people's nieces. At that point, I was very grateful for any kind of good advice. The consular officer advised that we take Cecil's body back for burial and offered assistance with the myriad of details, even coming to the airport four days later to see us off. He also retrieved Cecil's wedding band from the funeral home and gave it to Daniel, telling him to give it to me. Some of the embassy personnel even asked us to stay in their homes in town, but I felt more comfortable with the friends we had grown to love over the years. Already, many of our friends and acquaintances were dropping by the Harpers' home with condolences. It was like a non-stop four day visitation at a funeral home.

Mark arranged for us to go to our house on Saturday for, by then, we had decided to return to the U.S. once Cecil's body was released. When we arrived at the compound, many people had gathered, especially people from the bairro, our South African friends down the road, people from other missions, and people from the English-speaking church in town. They formed a huge prayer circle in the side yard, and many prayer walked around the property afterwards. One of our South African friends, Pastor Willie, had taken Daniel to the police station to identify one of the men they had caught. They arrived while we were still in the prayer circle. Then we went into the house, and Susan Brooks helped me take all the pictures out of our photo albums so that I could carry them back to the U.S. We packed everything we wanted to take back to the U.S. in suitcases. Deborah and I went back to Mark and Leslie's house. Daniel took the truck and went to stay with a friend in town.

The next morning, Sunday, Deborah went to the English-speaking church in town with the Harpers. Some of the young people took her to the bay in the afternoon as a farewell.

Daniel picked me up that morning to go back to the house one more time. As I stepped into the truck, Daniel said, "Mom, I want you to hear something."

"What?" I asked.

"I want you to hear what Dad was listening to in the truck before he came in Thursday night," he replied.

As he inserted the tape into the tape player, he said, "This tape was still in the tape deck when I took the truck."

It was the Chuckwagon Gang, singing about heaven. Every song on that tape was about heaven. Cecil died with heaven on his mind.

The next day, Monday, January 24, Daniel, Deborah, and I left to return to Kentucky. The embassy people met us at the Maputo airport and told us that they had learned that Cecil's casket would be held for inspection in South Africa. This meant we would not arrive with it after all. The headmaster from Trichardt School also met us with school records for the children and a letter of recommendation for me. Of course, the Harpers were there and many other friends and loved ones from Mozambique.

Dennis and Linda Messimer met us in Johannesburg where we had a layover before changing planes to Miami. They bought Daniel a rugby shirt in the South African colors. He wore it proudly for many months.

Dennis helped me exchange money, and then we got on the plane. For some reason, I was cold. I remember shivering. I couldn't stop shaking, and I didn't have any warm clothes. I bundled up in the blanket that the stewardess gave me, and the stewardess kept giving me hot drinks. I remember walking through the tunnel from the plane when we landed in Miami.

When we got to Louisville, our forwarding agents, my sister and her husband, and the three older children and their families met us. At my request, they had not allowed any reporters know when we were arriving. My sister had brought coats for Daniel, Deborah, and me -- so very thoughtful and far-thinking of her. My hair was a disaster, but Miriam promised that she would make sure that was rectified.

Ben had asked Louisville Bible College if we could borrow their van so that we could all be together. They graciously agreed. All five children, spouses, and grandchildren fit.

When we were all seated, Ben said, "Mom, we just want you to know that this tragic death of our dad will not destroy our faith. That's what we want you to know first of all."

How did he know that those were the most comforting words he could have uttered? I had fretfully worried, *What will this do to the children? Will they turn their backs on God? Will they think He's forsaken us?* Then we prayed and left the airport together, all in one vehicle.

Ben took us to Mrs. Johnstone's house, where Katie and he were living while Katie took care of the mother of a dear family friend at Fairdale Christian Church. The Johnstones graciously opened the large house to us and other relatives who were traveling in for the funeral. Cecil's body arrived a couple of days later, and the first night of visitation was January 27, Daniel's eighteenth birthday. He spent it at the funeral home with lots and lots of people.

Funeral and the Day After

Saturday, the day of the funeral, was a very snowy day. The service was a time of celebration, but I remember the dreary ride to the Rest Haven cemetery because it was a very cloudy, very overcast day. The Okolona church building was packed with people, and many stayed afterwards for the dinner the church provided.

The next day I returned to the same church building for worship. I remember sitting on the first row in the balcony. We sang the song, "I Will Never Be the Same Again." And I knew I never would!

Cedar Grove

The Johnstone family (for whom Ben's wife Katie worked) had a connection to one of the deacons at Cedar Grove Baptist Church in Shepherdsville, KY. Their parsonage at Cedar Grove was empty. The church invited Daniel, Kathy, Deborah, and me to move in for as long as we needed. We gratefully took them up on that offer and, not long after the funeral, we moved in. The parsonage was very, very nice. It had a garage, a big, open living room/kitchen/dining room, three bedrooms and two bathrooms – plenty of space for the four of us. God had provided for our immediate need for housing!

Lifting Up My Eyes

One of the best things about the parsonage at Cedar Grove was that it was located on top of a hill overlooking the church building, which had a cross as a steeple. Every morning, I would open the curtains of the big picture and see that cross framed against the hills. And every day, I would think, "I lift up my eyes to the hills-- where does my help come from? My help comes from the Lord, the Maker of Heaven and earth." (Psalm 121:1,2)

Then I would go over to my computer desk and open my computer. Every day, for three solid months, I would find a message from my friend in Papua New Guinea. Sharran, being 12 hours ahead of Kentucky in time, would write out the prayer that she prayed for me that morning. Through Sharran and the cross framed against the hills, God supplied my need for help, comfort, and encouragement.

Teapot Prayers

The upside and the downside of the parsonage at Cedar Grove was that it was way off my beaten path. While it provided a haven of peace and solitude, it also lent itself to a few lonely days. Almost everyone I knew, both in Shepherdsville and Louisville, worked during the day. The cold winter evenings did not encourage night-time visiting. I was used to living on a compound in the middle of a bairro in Mozambique with people everywhere all the time. The missionary wives on the compound got together in the late afternoons to drink tea and pray for our husbands, children, and different aspects of the work in which our families were involved.

One day, in the middle of a lonely Shepherdsville morning, I crossed my arms and grumbled to myself, "I don't even have anybody to drink tea with!"

I call that my complaining prayer. God heard it and answered it anyhow.

Late in the afternoon, a lady (I do not know her name) knocked on the front door. She said she was a member at Southeast Christian Church and had read the story of my husband's death in the Southeast Outlook. In her arms, she was holding a big basket with many varieties of special teas in it. In the middle of the basket was the prettiest little china teapot I had ever seen. God was listening, and He cared so much!

Cooper Avenue

In May, the people who were living in Okolona's mission house returned to their field of service, and we were invited by the church to move in. We had been the first family to live in this house when it opened in 1983 and had spent a total of five years of furlough time in it between 1983 and 2000. As much as we loved the peace and solitude of Cedar Grove, we were very eager to move back to familiar territory, close to our friends, family, and church that we loved. Okolona graciously allowed us to live in this house until June, 2007, when God provided the means to purchase a home of my own.

Closing the Good News for Africa Account

At the end of 2000, I sent letters to all of the people who had generously supported our family throughout twenty-four years of missionary service. I knew that many would be happy to continue financial support, but I did not feel right about that. I had a teaching degree; I could earn a living. I had been advised not to make any quick, rash decisions about my future immediately after Cecil's death. I am very grateful for the eleven months I had to pay bills, communicate with supporting churches, speak, and write. What a blessing!

Teaching in Kentucky

I substitute taught from January through May of 2001 at various schools, just to get my feet wet a little at a time. In the fall of 2001, I accepted a position as fourth grade teacher at Valor Traditional Academy and continued teaching in that position until beginning work at Team Expansion's International Services office in August, 2006. Those were happy days which I enjoyed to the utmost.

Team Expansion

In January of 2005, while still at Valor, I came to the realization that I had never asked God what He wanted me to do with the rest of my life. Even when we left Mozambique, I believe it was a rational decision without much time seeking God's input. For months before Cecil's death, I had been silently grieving the fact that Daniel would leave for college soon. Each time we were separated from a child, my heart broke again. I didn't think I could face this separation one more time.

So I said to Cecil, "Don't you think we should go home?" That was the first time I'd ever said that in my whole life.

He replied, "Just give me five more years."

So, when Cecil died, there wasn't much question in my mind whether I should go or stay. I thought I should go because of the other children who were already in the U.S., because of Daniel's impending departure, and because I didn't think Mozambique was a place for a single woman and a 13-year-old girl on their own. We'd be too much trouble for the other missionaries to have to look after and not that valuable to the work of training church leaders. I could still teach school, but that really was not the critical path of the mission. The critical path of the mission at that was to establish a training center and to train leaders for local churches. I was not involved in that, so it seemed like no question at all that I should go home.

When I did get home, I thought, "OK, Betty, you've got a teaching degree; so, of course, that's what you'll do to make a living."

To this day, I doubt that I asked God about that; but in 2005, I began to think about that.

I started asking God "Is this you want me to do with the rest of my life? I love teaching. I like this school."

I wasn't making a whole lot of money, and I was working two other jobs besides that; so it was a bit of a stretch financially.

But I thought, "I don't mind teaching. I don't mind tutoring at Sylvan. I don't mind being a mentor for new teachers in Kentucky. I can keep on like this."

Then I thought, "Maybe it's about time I should start asking God."

So, I started asking God. Two months later, the missions chairman said to me, "Did you see the prayer request in Horizons magazine? Team Expansion is looking for a prayer coordinator. Why don't you apply for that, Betty? That's what you do for the church."

Well, actually, it wasn't really what I did for the church. All I did was send out mission prayer requests to the Sunday school classes.

To make a very long story short, however, I inquired, eventually applied, was accepted, raised support, and began working full time as Prayer Coordinator for Team Expansion in August, 2006, and that's where God has me to this day.

Pressing On

"Not that I have already obtained all, or have already been made perfect, but I press on to take hold of that for which Christ Jesus took hold of me. Brothers, I do not consider myself yet to have taken hold of it. But this one thing I do: Forgetting what is behind and straining toward what is ahead, I press on toward the goal to win the prize for which God has called me heavenward in Christ Jesus." (Philippians 3:12-14 NIV)